Bullshit Baffles Brains

Front cover photograph: Ploughing the fields in front of San Wai Camp
Back cover photograph: The Dorsets on exercise in the New Territories supported by Comet tanks

Dedication

For all the Hong Kong Dorsets, and in memory of their remarkable Commanding Officer, Lieutenant-Colonel Geoffrey White DSO - 'Knocker'.

Bullshit Baffles Brains

An Account of the Dorsets in Hong Kong 1952 - 54

by Dick Eberlie and Christopher Jary

When the Chinese land on the Hong Kong strand
Then the Dorsets, they will make them stand,
With a tin of Brasso in each hand.
Oh the bullshit baffles brains!
When at last we reach Korea
The enemy will flee in fear
For our green hose-tops will appear.
Oh the bullshit baffles brains!
The wars were won oftentimes
By cavalry charges and thin red lines,
But we win ours by painting signs.
Oh the bullshit baffles brains!

Major Ivor Ramsay
OC Support Company, 1st Battalion, The Dorset Regiment, 1952-54

© 2015 Dick Eberlie and Christopher Jary

The right of Dick Eberlie and Christopher Jary to be identified as authors of this work has been asserted by them in accordance with the Copyright, Designs and Patents Act 1988.

A CIP catalogue record for this book is available from the British Library.

All rights reserved. No part of this book may be reproduced or transmitted in any form or by any means electronic or mechanical including photo-copying, recording or by any information storage and retrieval system, without permission from the authors in writing.

First Printing, 2015

ISBN 978-0-99290331-2

Produced in the United Kingdom by Bluemoon Print & Promotions.

Contents

	Acknowledgements	vii
Chapter 1	National Service, Hong Kong and the 1st Dorsets' Arrival at San Wai Camp *by Christopher Jary*	1
Chapter 2	Joining the Army *by Dick Eberlie*	19
Chapter 3	Hong Kong: Soldiering *by Dick Eberlie*	43
Chapter 4	Hong Kong: Social Life and Leisure *by Dick Eberlie*	91
Chapter 5	Hong Kong 1953-54 *by Christopher Jary*	135
Chapter 6	Memories *compiled by Christopher Jary*	149
Appendix 1	The Dorset Regimental Hymn and Collect	167
Appendix 2	Order of Battle of the 1st Battalion, The Dorset Regiment, 1952 and 1954	169
	Glossary	171
	Index	173

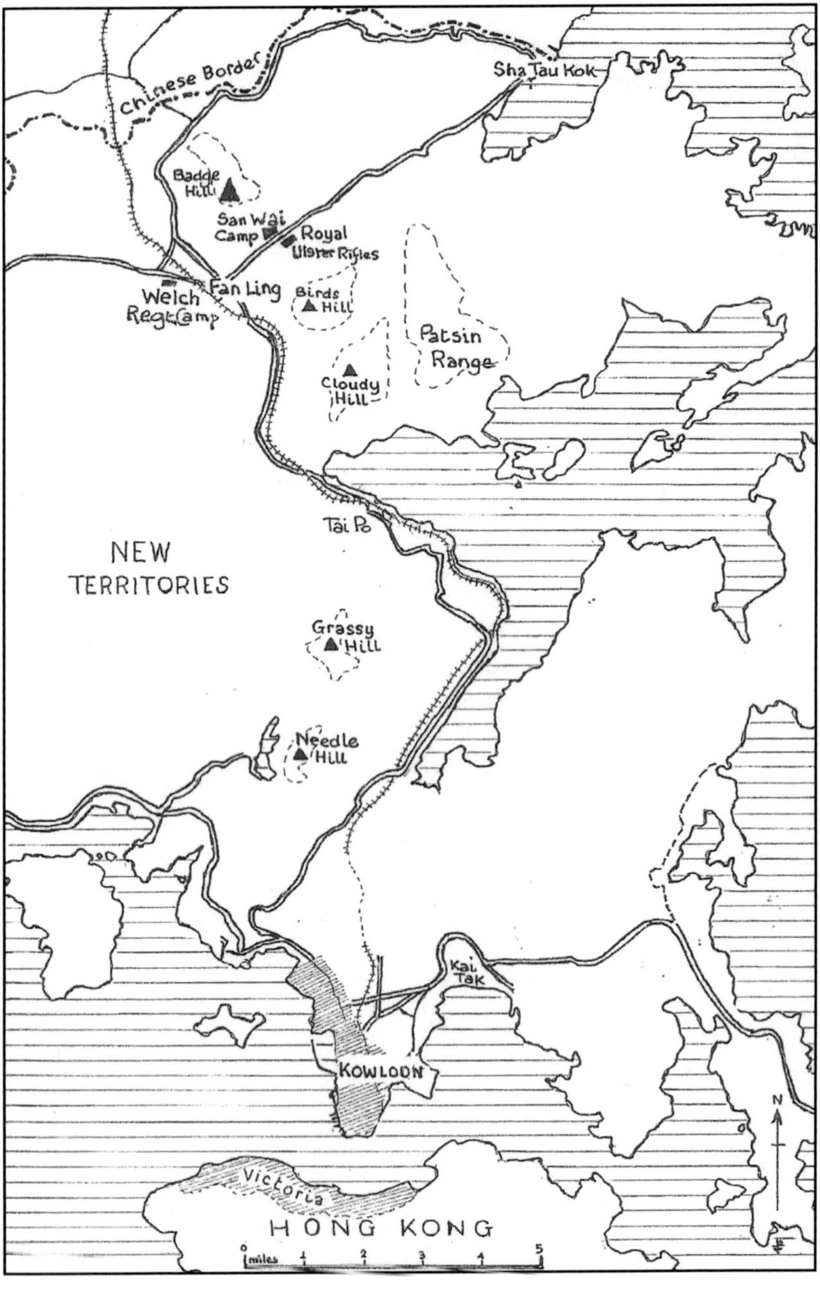

Chinese Border
Sha Tau Kok
Badge Hill
San Wai Camp
Royal Ulster Rifles
Fan Ling
Welch Regt Camp
Birds Hill
Patsin Range
Cloudy Hill
Tai Po
NEW TERRITORIES
Grassy Hill
Needle Hill
Kai Tak
KOWLOON
Victoria
HONG KONG
N
0 1 2 3 4 5
miles

Acknowledgements

This book owes its existence to Major Nick Speakman MBE TD. It was his idea, and he then did much of the research and most of the work involved in its publication. Without Nick, it would not have happened.

We should also like to thank the following who provided evocative photographs and vivid memories:

Michael Barton	Happy Harman	Frank Read
Patrick Burgess	Rex Hitchens	Bob Reep
David Chant	Gos Home	Colin Shortis
Stan Coombes	John Ives	Abe Stanley
John Curl	Donald Knight	Alf Tizzard
Tiddler Damon	Peter Lane	Richard Vater
Mike Davis-Sellick	Tony Marsh	Len Webb
Horace Dibben	Klaus Marx	Ron Webb
Geoff Eavis	Mrs Bill Osmond	
Jeff Eckersall	Gordon Pratten	

We are very grateful to Peter Turner, who drew the map of the New Territories, and to Colin Parr, Peter Metcalfe and John Murphy, who all helped with the photographs. We very much appreciated the access Chris Copson, the Keep Military Museum's Curator, allowed us to the Museum's archives.

Finally our thanks are due to Ben and Matthew Clark at Bluemoon, who oversaw the production process, and to Joan Eberlie and Lois Jary, who between them read every page and uncomplainingly shared their homes (and their husbands' attention) with this book for months on end.

Dorsets at San Wai Camp

Chapter 1

National Service, Hong Kong and the 1st Dorsets' Arrival at San Wai Camp

Say, soldier! Tell us the tricks,
the tackle of your trade;
The passage of your hours;
the plans that you have made -
Of what do you think - what consider?
Tell us of the slow process,
That gradual change -
from man to soldier - ?

From *Tell Us The Tricks* by Paul Scott

This book tells the story of the 1st Battalion, The Dorset Regiment, who were based at San Wai Camp in Hong Kong's New Territories from October 1952 until August 1954. Most of it was written by Dick Eberlie and originally formed part of his own memoirs. Chapters Two, Three and Four describe his initial training with the Essex Regiment and his time as a young subaltern with the Dorsets in England and in Hong Kong. The son of a general practitioner in Luton who had served in the Royal Navy during the First World War, Dick's lifelong links with Dorset began as a pupil at Sherborne School. Drawing on his diary, the letters he wrote home and a prodigious memory, he has produced a vivid story of a time, now more than six decades ago, when our young men were required to perform two years' National Service, when our soldiers were fighting the Chinese Army in Korea and communist bandits in Malaya, and when Britain had yet to withdraw from its last imperial commitments around the world.

In recent years, National Service has been the subject of several studies and has frequently figured as a chapter in the biographies and autobiographies of members of the generation born in the late 1920s and 1930s. For a nation which had never in peacetime adopted conscription, it amounted to an extraordinary social experiment established by a truly radical government. For those who served, it provided a unique experience which coloured their transition to adulthood and cost some their young lives. For the armed forces who received them, it was probably a mixed blessing: it swelled their numbers and attracted brighter recruits but ultimately diluted their professionalism.

Participants' responses to National Service varied enormously. A few loved it, a few loathed and resented it; most gained something from the experience - even if sometimes that something was simply the pride of having endured it. While writing the story of the Dorset Regiment I was privileged to meet and get to know a number of their National Servicemen from the late 1940s and 1950s who now comprise the vast majority of the Regiment's Old Comrades. In 2013 on the beach at Weymouth I mentioned this to an officer from another regiment who expressed great surprise that any National Servicemen had maintained contact with their regiment. None from his regiment, he told me, ever attended reunions. The Dorsets seem different and it is worth considering why.

Many National Servicemen who endured the experience without enthusiasm remember it as a purposeless existence in what seemed an alien - if temporary - environment; their officers were remote, often invisible beings and some of their NCOs were bullies. This was not the lot of the Dorsets' young soldiers, who found themselves absorbed into a new regimental family founded on strong links to the county. A boy from Dorchester, Sherborne, Gillingham or Poole would soon gravitate to others from the same town. These links are still evident today at Old Comrades' gatherings where a distinct geographical distribution remains discernible among the tables! Dorset's social cohesion extended to National Service. The Dorset Regiment of the 1950s was still the county in uniform.

Basic training could be hard. Dick Eberlie's feelings in September 1950 when he joined the Essex Regiment at Colchester would have been common to many conscripts, although his personal experience was also coloured by his years at Sherborne School. Ex-public schoolboys usually found that their education had inured them to homesickness - which hit many National Servicemen hard in their first weeks - and that service in their schools' Combined Cadet Force had provided a head start in drill, weapons handling and service discipline. But that education had also been an experience that was far removed from the childhoods most of their contemporaries had led and the civilian futures that lay ahead. The public schoolboys' different accents, manner and attitudes made them conspicuous and often hampered communication with young men from other backgrounds. But, for many men of all sorts and conditions, basic training must have been an ordeal. Those strange, rigorous twelve weeks were hard for everyone as each adjusted to army life and to the array of different men in his intake.

Acquiring some sense of purpose became easier when each joined a unit. In this, recruits joining the 1st Dorsets in 1952 were perhaps fortunate. The Battalion had a clear role to perform, an interesting posting in an exotic location and a strong sense of purpose. In Hong Kong the Battalion were training other soldiers to join the war in Korea and were themselves expecting to follow them into battle. Only a year earlier that war had cost the life of John Milner, a young Dorset officer serving with the Argylls. Another, Alan Blundell, remained a prisoner of the Chinese alongside several other Dorsets who had all been captured fighting with the Glosters on the Imjin River.

Their sense of purpose was heightened by the impressive experience, professionalism and leadership of their officers, warrant officers and NCOs. Their first Colonel, Tom Affleck-Graves, was an accomplished and very experienced staff officer, who had commanded HQ Company of the 2nd Dorsets during the Phoney War. Sadly, he was taken ill on the voyage to Hong Kong and, soon after their arrival, had to be sent home. His successor, Geoffrey *Knocker* White, was a legendary fighting soldier, who had fought at Kohima and won the Distinguished Service Order commanding the 2nd Dorsets throughout the rest of the campaign in Assam and Burma. Their Training Officer was Bill Heald, a Dorset who in the Italian campaign had won a DSO and a Military Cross commanding a platoon, a company and briefly a battalion of Hampshires.

Major Rupert Wheatley, who joined the Battalion in Hong Kong and became Second in Command, was a third generation Dorset who had won a DSO near Arnhem, leading a company of a Wiltshire battalion he later commanded. Among the company commanders were other wartime veterans including Ivor Ramsay, who fought with the 2nd Battalion in France in 1940, John Smith - known as *J B* - who had led Sikhs in Burma, and John Freer-Smith, whose humane, kindly and effective leadership is still remembered by those lucky enough to have served under him. The Adjutant was the highly professional John Archer, who had served his apprenticeship as White's Adjutant in 1946 and would rise meteorically to become Commander-in-Chief, UK Land Forces. The RSM was the towering John Webber, who had been captured on Hill 112 with the 4th Dorsets and had served with the Life Guards. Among the Warrant Officers were Jimmy James, who had won the MM with the 2nd Dorsets during the retreat to Dunkirk and who would succeed Mr Webber as Regimental Sergeant-Major, and Orderly Room Quartermaster Sergeant Ted Ralph, who had twenty-eight years' service and had served with the 1st Battalion in India, Malta and Sicily. Among the Sergeants was Len Metcalfe, who had won the Military Medal with the 5th Dorsets in North West Europe. Experience had taught them what counted in battle, and what did not. Such men did not resort to, or tolerate, bullying. Their professionalism permeated the whole Battalion.

Knocker White himself was a distinguished battlefield commander, a demanding colonel and a second generation, devoted Dorset who took immense pains to get to know not only his officers, but also his men. Himself an Olympic standard athlete, he encouraged his soldiers in all forms of sport, and his encouragement fuelled the Battalion's spectacular performance in this respect. From the Commanding Officer's point of view, sport was triply beneficial. It enabled his Battalion to shine, developed his soldiers' fitness and consumed young men's energy that otherwise might have been misspent. Colonel White may perhaps have had more energy than was likely to make him relaxing company but he devoted all he had single-mindedly and selflessly to the service of his Regiment, his Battalion and his soldiers. He drove them - officers and men - as hard as he drove himself, setting and attaining a high standard of professionalism in all things. By chance, the bound copies of the Regimental Journals I have drawn on for my parts of this book were once his. The flyleaf bears his signature and the contents bear his frequent annotations, carefully correcting tiny errors and highlighting news items about fellow Dorsets with whom he had served. White had a powerful sense of the continuity of regimental history, which he lived, breathed and communicated at every opportunity to his soldiers. Under him they learned and celebrated what it meant to be a Dorset - *Primus in Indis* and Plassey, Marabout, the *Sarah Sands*, Tirah, La Bassée, Kut-al-Amara, Festubert, Sicily, Kohima, D-Day, Arnhem and Dorset Wood - all were remembered and marked by the men under his command. The battles were re-enacted at tattoos, remembered on anniversaries and even described in their Colonel's orders of the day. The Regiment's past ran like an unbreakable thread through the daily life of this modern Battalion.

The Dorsets' experience presents a powerful case for the flexibility and inclusivity of our county regiments. In the Second World War - which ended only seven years before this book begins - the fighting battalions of the Regiment had several times absorbed platoons and even whole companies from other regiments. Injections of Durham Light Infantrymen, Glosters, men from the Bedfordshire and Hertfordshire Regiment, Gunners and Canadians had brought them not just numbers but new qualities to complement their own. In Burma and in Normandy the Dorsets had learned the value of such inclusivity, which profited them again when they were joined in Hong Kong by a substantial draft of Royal Fusiliers. Among these Fusiliers was Lieutenant Colin Shortis, who (after fighting with his own Regiment in Korea) quickly transferred to the Dorsets and rose to command the 1st Devon and Dorsets before ultimately becoming their Colonel. His experience as a Royal Fusilier officer joining the 1st Dorsets will be described in the last chapter. War experience had taught Colonel White not just the benefits of the Battalion as a strong family unit, but also the importance of the extended family beyond that unit. Throughout his time in Hong Kong he was tireless in building strong, working relationships between the 1st Dorsets and their supporting Gunners, Sappers, armour and even the other two services.

This inclusivity extended to individual National Servicemen, some of whom in civilian life had faced hardship or tragedy. One such was Private Patrick Burgess, who in August 1952 lost six members of his family - including the grandmother who had brought him up - in the Lynmouth Flood. Arriving in

Hong Kong, he later remembered *I was still very much bereaved and was not behaving properly and soon found myself in trouble. Captain Freer-Smith showed much understanding and compassion when I should have been in serious trouble. I can see now why he was [later] Families Officer for 1st Devon and Dorsets and was awarded the MBE for his excellent work.*

What emerges from the story of the 1st Dorsets at this time is a portrait of a remarkable Commanding Officer working tirelessly to build on the foundations of young National Servicemen a professional battalion that he could take to war. In the company of fellow Dorsets and in an environment dominated by the example of their officers, warrant officers and NCOs, it was difficult for any of them to lack a sense of purpose and every bit as difficult not to acquire a sense of belonging to a fine Battalion who were heirs to a proud tradition. This atmosphere permeates Dick Eberlie's memories and shines through those of the other Dorsets who have contributed their stories to the first and final parts of this book.

⊕ ⊕ ⊕

The post-war world this book describes now seems another age and, like National Service, it attracts wide popular interest in 21st Century Britain. Those times saw the transition from Empire to Commonwealth, from the threat from Hitler's Germany to the threat from Stalin's Russia, and from Britain as a world power to Britain as a partner with America and many European nations within NATO. Victory in the Second World War had weakened and almost bankrupted Great Britain. By 1946 a seismic shift in the global balance of power had begun the Cold War, a brooding, hostile stand-off in which a western alliance of democracies led by the United States of America faced a Communist bloc centred on Russia's Soviet Union.

In the post-war years Great Britain's straitened domestic finances and the transformed international scene required a policy of peaceful disengagement from Empire. Events moved swiftly. 1947 brought the partition of India, British withdrawal and the creation of two new independent and, sadly, hostile states: India and Pakistan. The following year saw the end of the British mandate in Palestine and the arrival of the infant state of Israel, a home for the Jews, surrounded by Arab states keen to strangle it at birth. The same year saw the start of a twelve-year commitment by British forces to prevent Communist-inspired attempts to seize Malaya. 1949 witnessed Mao Tse Tung's revolution in China and the creation of a second massive and despotic Communist state. Mao's attitude to Britain and the western democracies was made clear in April when his People's Liberation Army fired on and immobilised the British warship HMS *Amethyst* when she was making peaceful passage up the Yangtse River. Escalation was averted when happily, after three months, despite damage and casualties, *Amethyst* slipped silently in darkness through the Chinese forces and rejoined the Fleet. Great Britain's relations with China deteriorated further when Mao's government sent a huge army to support Communist North Korea in the Korean War and, in April 1951, launched a massive offensive against the South Korean and United Nations forces there.

In Africa the tide of withdrawal from Empire continued. In 1951 the British release of Nkrumah from prison on the Gold Coast allowed major shifts in the Colony's constitution that led to peaceful independence and the creation of Ghana six years later. Political unrest in Egypt led to the overthrow of the Egyptian monarchy in 1953, heralding both the Suez Crisis of 1956 and the independence of the Sudan.

While the tide of Empire receded across Africa and Asia, the tiny, distant Colony of Hong Kong remained unmoved. A Crown Colony held by the British on a ninety-nine-year lease granted by China in 1898, Hong Kong's position was unique. In British hands since 1842, the Colony had developed quite independently of mainland China, from which it had received influxes of immigrants. Immigration had peaked in the 1930s during the savage Japanese attack on China. During the war Hong Kong had itself been captured by the Japanese and had suffered all the brutality - execution, deportation, rape, starvation and disease - that attended occupation by the Japanese. Its population had fallen to 600,000, which was less than half its pre-war strength. Since the Communist Revolution in China another influx of immigration had begun. This offered the Colony the prospect of a new prosperity, based on the renewed importance of a free port on the China Sea and the availability of cheap labour for Hong Kong's textile industry. But it brought also the threat of over-population and saw the rapid growth of huge squatter camps flimsily and dangerously constructed from cast-off materials that would be swept away by the monsoon rain or the gusts of the next typhoon.

This was the environment the 1st Dorsets encountered when they arrived in late October 1952 and which Dick Eberlie describes so vividly in his memoir. They arrived at a delicate time in Sino-British relations. The two nations were still fighting in Korea and, as we have seen, some Dorsets remained prisoners of the Chinese. Negotiations were in progress to end hostilities without the West having to resort to the atomic bomb. The Dorsets had four principal duties in the Colony: to undertake ceremonial duties and show the flag; to train troops and prepare themselves to fight in Korea; to police Hong Kong's borders; and to defend the Colony against attack. The last of these - with the apparently limitless People's Liberation Army just the other side of the border - was quite impossible. Happily it did not prove necessary. We know now that the 1st Dorsets were not called upon to fight in Korea, that the Dorset prisoners were returned maltreated but alive, and that the Korean War did not end in atomic Armageddon. But no one knew that at the time, when these threats loomed large over the young men who served there.

The year 1952 was a memorable one for the Dorset Regiment, marking the 250th anniversary of the creation of the 39th Regiment of Foot in Ireland. January found the 1st Battalion still in Austria, where they had been since early 1948, but plans were being made there and in Dorchester to make the anniversary a memorable occasion. The death of King George VI on 6th February 1952 caused the celebrations to be postponed but, five months later, the new Queen visited the Depot in Dorchester and, for the only time in history, the Royal Standard flew above the Keep. The Regiment's anniversary commemorations began in Dorset and in Vienna, where command of the 1st Battalion had passed from Lieutenant-Colonel Tim Wood to Lieutenant-Colonel Tom Affleck-Graves. In July Affleck-Graves brought his Battalion back to England. Here at Chiseldon Camp they received 350 new soldiers and their new CO faced in a very few weeks the huge task of preparing his command for imminent service in the Far East. It was there that Dick Eberlie joined them and played a part in one of the last events before they left: a dramatic tattoo, organised by Knocker White at the Depot in Dorchester, to mark the Regiment's anniversary.

The Advance Party of the 1st Dorsets sailed from Liverpool aboard HM Troopship *Empire Pride* in the late summer. Among their number was twenty-five-year-old Corporal (later Sergeant) *Spud* Taylor, who as a teenager had served in Normandy and North West Europe with the 12th (Airborne) Battalion of the Devonshire Regiment. Discharged after an exciting and dangerous war, he had re-enlisted and joined the 1st Dorsets in Vienna. Now, keen to serve in the Far East, he had volunteered to join the Advance Party. In his memoirs he recalled the cramped conditions of the mess decks aboard the troopship.

There were a number of long fixed tables which seated about twenty men on fixed benches. Three men from each table were detailed to report to the galley at meal times, and they collected the food for their own particular table; the food was served out at the end and passed along the table until everyone was served. Unequal serving portions meant that sometimes those who were the last to receive their meal might get short rations, so that there was great interest and minute observation frequently followed by intense argument if the distribution had not seemed to be fair.

After the meals the tables were cleaned up and, if there were no other parades or duties, the men used those same tables to write letters, play games, read or just yarn to one another. It was only after the last parades, or 8.30pm, that hammocks were allowed to be slung. That rule had to be strictly observed otherwise it would not be possible to move around the mess deck. The height of the deck was about seven feet, and once slung the hammock hung down from the fixtures below the deck head about three to four feet so there was only about one foot of room between the hammock and the table top…

Imagine if you can the pandemonium at hammock slinging time! Everyone struggling, pushing and fighting to be the first to claim the best places. These were near to the gangways and ventilation points which were the coolest places to sleep. It was also a comparatively easy matter to move, to get out of the hammock to visit the heads [lavatories]. It was quite another matter if one was placed against the side of the deck away from the exits or, even worse, somewhere in the middle of that seething mass, because to visit the toilets one would have to turn the hammock over whilst still in it, and then upside down put one's hands down on to the table, lower oneself down and crawl along under the swinging hammocks to the nearest exit or gangway where it might be possible to stand up again.

…During the day life was not too bad, but at night it was chaotic. We were so

packed in that there were only a few inches between the hammocks and they were slung head to foot in rows. It was almost necessary at night to shout out 'all turn' and a whole row of men could turn over and ease their aching limbs. Often they were so tightly jammed together that it was impossible to move unless someone else did so first.

Curses were uttered as the men were woken by the bumping and pushing of those unlucky ones who were furthest from the gangways and, as they pushed and shoved and forced their way under and through the hammocks to get out, tempers would become frayed and fights break out, then things would quieten down for a while until another man had to relieve himself and the process would be repeated. It was not exactly luxury cruising, but the normal method of transporting troops around the Empire.

... This particular journey was a six-week trip. ... To keep fit there were daily physical exercises and games. The boredom was relieved by quite unnecessary training and cleaning parades.

After welcome stops at Gibraltar, Malta and Port Said, HMT *Empire Pride* took a day to navigate the Suez Canal before emerging into the Red Sea. At Aden Taylor remembered *one of the cooks came up on deck and threw a box of food scraps and leftovers from the evening meal over the side. I watched it as it slowly drifted along the hull of the anchored vessel and was surprised to see a large shark that came close to eat the food scraps.... It was about twelve feet long and I had never been as close to one before... just looking down on it from the deck was frightening.*

The scorching searing heat in the Red Sea was intense. It was torture as we sweated our way through it; the old hands who had experienced a number of passages through said that summer or winter made no difference; the heat was always the same and one got no respite from it. We were given permission to sling our hammocks on deck to catch what air there was; for those still sleeping on the mess deck it must have been suffocating. It took three and a half days before we entered the cooler waters of the Indian Ocean.

I found the voyage quite pleasant now and I spent hours leaning over the rail near the bow, watching the flying fish as they left the water and sped along just above the waves sometimes for a hundred yards or more before diving back into the sea...

I enjoyed watching the dolphins, too, as they sped along in the bow wave of the ship, criss-crossing the bow and occasionally jumping three or four feet in the air, always in perfect unison with the others.

Dormitory aboard a troopship

Troops' dining room aboard a troopship

After stops at Colombo and Singapore, the ship arrived at Hong Kong and Taylor and the rest of the Advance Party moved to San Wai Camp to prepare for the arrival of the Battalion.

On the morning of Saturday 4th October 1952, the main party of the 1st Dorsets embarked at Southampton on HMT *Empire Fowey*. A large party arrived to see them off and to wish them well on their journey and in their new station. Among them was the Colonel of the Regiment Brigadier Charles Woodhouse, Colonel Steve (who had commanded the 2nd Battalion at Dunkirk), Councillor Edward Hedger the Mayor of Dorchester, Lieutenant-Colonels Os Ball, Speedy Bredin and Knocker White, and a number of vintage Dorsets - Messrs Richards, Morris, Cavell and Stevens who (like Os Ball) had all enlisted before the First World War. The senior among them, Mr Richards, had enlisted in 1899. It was a homely send-off provided by some very distinguished old friends as well as friends and families of many of the Dorsets on board. The Band played as, at 1220, their troopship cast off into the Channel.

The weather frowned upon them. Continuous fog slowed their passage south and delayed their arrival at Gibraltar. Near Malta they changed into tropical kit only to suffer the coldest day of the voyage with heavy rain and thunder. In the Red Sea despite the extreme heat the Battalion persisted with their full daily programme, which began at 0630 with a twenty-minute PT session. Many remember as the most enjoyable aspect of the voyage the shooting sessions run by Major Ivor Ramsay and Second Lieutenant Dick Eberlie. Crates were thrown overboard into the wash of the ship and were raked with rifle, Sten and Bren gun fire.

They stopped at Colombo and again at Singapore, where they were entertained by two Dorset officers - Lieutenant-Colonels Tim Wood and Skinny Laugher - who were stationed there, but the heavens opened and the party-goers were drenched as they returned to their ship. Lieutenant-Colonels Sam Symes and the recently promoted Knocker White, who had just arrived to take command of a Malayan battalion, were unable to join them but sent their apologies and greetings.

The 1st Battalion docked at Kowloon in the morning of 31st October and were met by representatives of the Advance Party, who reported that all was well at San Wai Camp. The last part of their journey was by train up into the New

HMT Empire Fowey

Territories to Fan Ling.

Spud Taylor remembered their new camp, which *lay at the foot of Badge Hill, the whole face of it covered with large cut-out replicas of the cap badges of the various regiments that had been stationed there. These were quite big and could be seen for miles...*

The camp consisted of Quonset huts, lined half round buildings of corrugated iron, which were pinned to the ground with two steel cables which passed over the top of the huts and were fixed firmly in the ground. The frequent typhoons could lift a building like a toy and carry it off if they were not fixed by the cables. One of these storms had lifted a large cruise liner and deposited it two miles inland such was its terrible power. Everything would grind to a halt at these times and people would just stay indoors and wait out the storm...

San Wai Camp, which would be the Battalion's home for the next two years, won no architectural awards. Built of prefabricated huts, its only permanent building was the concrete block of squash courts. The surrounding country was spectacular. To the north, beyond the hills, lay Communist China. To

Battalion on Parade below Badge Hill

the south lay Kowloon and Hong Kong Island. The climate brought extreme heat, monsoon rain and frequent typhoons. Mosquitoes carried malaria and all ranks had to take paludrin tablets every day. It seemed as if the young men from Dorset had stepped into a bygone era set in an ancient landscape. The surrounding fields were ploughed by bullocks driven by peasants in conical straw hats who spoke no English. Lieutenant Bob Reep remembered that, when out on exercise, the modern Battalion was supported by a troop of an Animal Pack Transport Company of the Royal Army Service Corps, whose mules and their handlers could carry supplies across country and up the steep, winding Jeep tracks to the Dorsets' operational positions.

Corporal Michael Barton, who arrived with the Battalion on the *Empire Fowey*, recalled San Wai Camp vividly.

It was divided by a small river, on one side HQ, A, B C and D Companies and the Sergeants', WOs' and Officers' accommodation, with muleteers nearby. On the other side Support Company, parade ground and Guardroom. Outside the perimeters were the sports ground and rifle range. The cookhouse lay in the middle

San Wai Camp

of the camp to which all traipsed with mug and utensils three times a day. It was advisable to get there early or at least be in advance of the hungry horde. The cooks had a difficult job to rustle up a tasty cuisine from the provisions. There were no real choices and the servers would splat food like mashed potato, stringy cabbage or other serving onto your plate. If one was late, apart from the lukewarm food and unclean tables, washing plates became a nauseous affair with the boiling cauldrons for rinsing resembling soup…

On the other side of the main road, in the Royal Ulsters' camp, was a cinema. At weekends a military transport service ran between our camp and Fan Ling railway station. Waiting for a train into Kowloon or for transport back was made easier by refreshments provided by a café known as 'The Better 'Ole' after a cartoon caption created by Captain Bruce Bairnsfather of the Royal Warwickshire Regiment during the First War.

Even here they still encountered echoes of home. Six thousand miles from his home in Dorchester, Private Jeff Eckersall's first encounter in Hong Kong was with a close friend from Dorset, who was serving with the 1st Wiltshires,

Monsoon flood

who were about to leave. The Dorsets joined 27 Brigade, commanded by Brigadier Bill Stirling, and served alongside the 1st Welch Regiment. Among the handful of other battalions in the Colony were the 1st Royal Ulster Rifles and the 1st Royal Norfolks, who were brigaded with the 2nd King Edward VII's Own Gurkha Rifles in Brigadier *Tiger* Urquhart's 35 Brigade. Corporal Horace Dibben remembered a football match against a Gurkha team, who played in bare feet. The presence of the Royal Norfolks was especially welcome. Since the campaign in Mesopotamia in 1915 when depleted battalions of the two regiments had formed a composite unit - the *Norsets* - there had been close links between the Dorsets and Royal Norfolks. Many *Norset* events would be held during their time in Hong Kong.

Spud Taylor recalled the Peak Railway on Hong Kong Island, which *travelled up and down to and from the peak. It was specially built for the one purpose and was very near to the vertical. It was a grand experience, and from the peak one got a breath-taking view of the Harbour and the New Territories.*

The waterfront at Kowloon

He found the Colony *a beautiful place with a thriving economy, but it was packed tight with people. The fact that the economy was booming and living conditions were far better than in China meant that the Chinese on the other side of the border were constantly trying to sneak into the New Territories and settle down and live the better life that was available there. The Police and border guards fought a continual battle to catch and return to China thousands of poor people who were striving to get away from the bad conditions in their own country.*

Inevitably quite a number made it through without detection and the population in the Colony was increasing rapidly all the time. These poorer citizens would take up residence on the hillsides close to the town, building themselves ramshackle shelters out of bits of tin and wood or even cardboard. These during the rainy season would collapse and be washed away, sometimes with loss of life.

Their upbringing had brought the young men of the early 1950s few opportunities to travel. Their childhoods had been darkened by war and their adolescence restricted by the Attlee Government's programme of austerity. For the 1st Battalion's National Servicemen arriving from Poole, Bridport or

Weymouth among strange sounds, exotic smells and unfamiliar sights must have seemed like landing on a distant planet. Some, like Geoff Eavis (who signed on for three years, later served in Korea and managed several trips to Japan), decided to make the most of this opportunity to see new places.

In his 2014 study of National Service, Professor Richard Vinen remarked that many of the ex-National Servicemen he interviewed still *looked back on service in Singapore or Hong Kong as the great adventure of their lives.* Many of the Dorset Regiment's Hong Kong veterans seem to share this view. *Bullshit Baffles Brains* attempts to portray some of their sense of adventure, and our next three chapters describe the personal experience of Private, later Lieutenant, Dick Eberlie. His story starts in September 1950 with his arrival, aged eighteen and fresh from Sherborne School, at the Depot of the Essex Regiment in Colchester.

Chapter 2

Joining the Army

Today we have naming of parts.
Yesterday we had daily cleaning and tomorrow morning
We shall have what to do after firing.
But today we have naming of parts.
     From *Lessons of the War* by Henry Reed

Colchester

The law of the land in 1950 required able-bodied men reaching the age of eighteen to serve two years in one of the armed forces. I travelled by bus from Sherborne to Salisbury to have a Medical Board on 20th July and was classified A1, so was obliged to set aside two years of my life in the service of King George VI.

I could have postponed National Service until after gaining my degree at university; and I could have chosen any of the three services, but, like most of my school-friends, I opted to go straight into the Army from school. I had no particular reasons for this choice, other than that everyone else was doing it and we all wanted to get the commitment over as fast as possible in order to resume normal life as soon as we could. I did not realise until much later the effect my decision would have on my father's plans for retirement. I naively assumed my scholarship would cover the expenses of my degree course, but the college told my father he would have to pay all my tuition fees in addition to my living allowance. There was no financial help from the Government in those days; so my father was aware he would have to continue working while I was at university in order to have the funds to cover my further education. He never mentioned this problem, however, when I was deciding what to do after leaving school.

My call-up papers reached me while I was sailing at Aldeburgh, and one week later, on 7th September 1950, I boarded the train at Liverpool Street on my way to Meeanee Barracks at Colchester. When I stepped off the train at the station, I was gathered up with several other men of my age and told to climb in the back of an army truck waiting to take us up to the barracks. They were the same ugly construction as all the others built in the Victorian age all over the country. They comprised several huge red-brick monstrosities that were our sleeping quarters, a wide parade ground of tarmac, a cookhouse and long lines of offices, messes and stores. At the grand entrance gates was the usual guard room with a sentry outside and the Essex Regiment's emblems and standards flying. I was to join the Depot of the Essex Regiment.

On arrival inside the gates, we were lined up at the quartermaster's stores

September 1950. Colchester. A Private in the Essex Regiment - hating every moment.

to receive army clothing and other kit, while the sergeants and corporals who would have charge of us introduced themselves. I joined fifty men in Number 4 Platoon of A Company. We were given beds and blankets in dormitories for fifteen men in the bare, draughty barrack blocks. We were then taken across to the cook-house for an evening meal, armed with mess tin, knife, spoon and fork. The food was passable, but the tea made with condensed milk was terrible, while washing our eating irons in a sink of filthy water on the way out of the cookhouse was very nasty.

My fellow recruits came from towns and villages in the three counties round the northern and eastern fringes of London. Most of them had had only a year or two's education after leaving primary school and had already been at work for some time as mechanics, technicians or labourers; and many seemed to have few interests outside the cinema, comics, popular music, and girls. Some had a small vocabulary with one or two words in constant use. They talked noisily to each other about their sexual adventures, and they swore every third word - as did the corporals and sergeants put in charge of us.

This was a totally new experience for me. About the worst word we ever used at school was "bloody"; I heard boastful old boys use one or two other words when they came back to revisit the school; and I knew enough about sex to be going on with, but I rapidly grew bored when these men talked of their girls far into the night. I loathed the swearing and the way some of them harped on sex, and I had little in common with them. I never found their companionship easy, and never enjoyed it, though I was able to live and let live. I got on reasonably happily with everyone - one morning offering to help someone with a problem, and the next day asking for help myself. So we rubbed along together, laughing at our discomforts and sharing our hearty dislike of the NCOs in charge of us.

Among my intake, six had enjoyed the same sort of background as mine; one chap had been to Gresham's School and won a scholarship to Selwyn College, Cambridge; another had been Head of Boxing at Oundle which earned him the respect of his fellows; and a third came from Potter Heigham on the Broads and was a keen sailor. Mike Dashwood had been to a small independent school at Sherbourne (with a u) in Gloucestershire, whom I was to meet later in the TA. Ray Hands was a pleasant, wiry man who subsequently distinguished himself winning an MC with the Suffolk Regiment in the Malayan jungle in the fight against the

Communist insurgents. Mike Casey became my closest friend at Colchester. He was a little chap with curly hair and a cheerful manner whose home was only a few miles from the Camp at the village of Layer de la Haye. Some of this small group foolishly patronised their room-mates and did not bother to try to fit in. Naturally they were unpopular, and some of them were given apple-pie beds one night which put them in serious trouble with the corporal.

Reveille was at 6.30am and we were woken even earlier on our first day by a corporal in heavy boots shouting at us to get up and out quickly. In great haste, we had to dress and put on our boots, make our beds, sweep the floor round them, try and find a basin in which to shave, run across to the cookhouse for a hurried breakfast, tear back and finish dressing and line up outside. Those who were slow were sworn at by the sergeant for being late on parade. We were then taken on visits to the dentist and doctor and given our first introduction to rifle drill, learning to respond when shouted at. The next morning we were made to line up at the barbers for a 'regimental haircut'. Most of our hair was cut off. I hated that, feeling that I looked like a convict, and was relieved to be able to persuade the barber not to smother my head in Brylcreme.

On our third day, more drill and P T were followed by a tour of the barracks, and a visit to the Medical Officer for a TAB1 injection which became increasingly painful as the day wore on. We went to bed at 8.30 in the evening and lay on our backs because both arms were so sore. We all had sick headaches and felt nausea, and drank nothing but tea. Yet one fellow droned on non-stop about his girls until three in the morning, so none of us had much sleep; and much of the following day we stayed in the noisy barrack-room with a wireless bellowing monotonous music, while shivering and aching with a stiff arm.

On our first Monday, the effects of the TAB wore off, and we were put through a variety of tests and interviews. We then began the routine of Spit and Polish that continued throughout my Colchester days. We were obliged constantly to work on our clothing and gear to smarten them up for regular inspections and parades. Our battle-dress tunics had to be precisely pressed, our uniform trousers to have perfect creases; our belts and spats to be covered evenly with khaki blanco, our buckles to shine so that you could see your face in them; our regimental cap badges to sparkle; and our boots to be polished with black boot polish and spit so that they too shone so that you could shave in them; and our rifles - our best friend, so we were told - to be oiled and cleaned endlessly to perfection. Our fingers and nails were covered all the time with boot polish, brasso and blanco.

Alongside this endless process of cleaning and polishing, rifle drill began in earnest on the parade ground. Early in the morning and late in the afternoons we had to do energetic physical exercises as well. We were taught how to salute officers and learned quickly to salute whenever we saw one. Otherwise we had little to do with them.

Gradually, the training became more interesting and perhaps more worthwhile. We were shown the parts of our .303 Lee Enfield rifles and endlessly made to practise loading and unloading, aiming and firing. We were introduced to the other weapons then used by infantrymen. The LMG or Bren gun was awkward to carry but a very valuable piece of equipment. The Sten gun was considered unreliable but handy in a scrap. The little .22 rifle was easy to use, but fired fairly harmless pellets. The cumbersome PIAT was fearfully heavy but supposedly capable of stopping a tank. We were taught discipline on the firing ranges and given the chance to fire our rifles and Brens there; we were given bayonet practice; and we were taken out into the countryside and started learning fieldcraft - how to dig trenches, how to use ground, how to camouflage ourselves. We were taken on route marches and on runs across the Essex countryside (which fortunately was flat in the area round the barracks). We went on just one cross-country run - at which I was pleased to find I did well, finishing among the leaders.

In all that we did, we were constantly harassed to respond promptly and correctly to the orders from the corporals, sergeants and sergeant majors. They took bullying to a fine art. They made sure they got a reaction from us by deliberately making themselves unpleasant. They harried us while we were struggling to get to grips with all this unaccustomed behaviour and strange equipment. On my sixth day I was 'checked', that is told off sharply and publicly shamed, for having a dirty rifle at the early morning inspection. The NCOs got the results they wanted, however; for after a few weeks, we began to work together as a platoon and to behave, move and think like soldiers.

The lowest moment of my Colchester service came after eight weeks when the whole Depot paraded in front of top brass. Orders were given by the Regimental

Sergeant Major whom everyone held in awe. Our platoon of new recruits was ordered to prepare itself for the big occasion; so we polished and cleaned as never before with the threat of unpleasant punishment if we failed to come up to the standards demanded by the sergeant major. We rehearsed the drill *ad nauseam* until we were heartily tired of it all. The big day came. Straining every nerve, we marched out into our place in the ranks; and we performed reasonably well. A gaggle of officers, the RSM and a bunch of sergeants then came forward to inspect us. They walked slowly along the front of each rank scrutinising each one of us carefully, as we stood rigidly to attention, not daring to blink an eyelid. They passed me without comment; I breathed a sign of relief. Then they chose to walk along the rank behind us equally slowly inspecting our backs; and when they came to me they paused. I heard mutterings and grunts and scribbling as someone wrote something down before they moved on. My heart was in my mouth; I was very worried indeed.

After the parade, I was called out by a sergeant and told I was 'on Company Orders' - that meant I was in deep trouble, but I was given no reason. I was ordered to report to the Company Office at such and such a time in my best battledress. More polishing and cleaning. I was truly terrified, when I was marched in before the officer.

"*Lef' ri' Lef' ri'! Tenshun! Orfcaps!*"

There I stood trembling. The officer said, "*Two two four o eight, six four eight, Private Everley, you are on a charge. You are charged that you were improperly dressed on parade in that you had a dirty neck.*" Never mind the grammar, I was aghast. This was none of the usual soldiers' crimes, like a dirty cap badge, or dull boots. This was unheard of and thoroughly unsavoury. I was ashamed of myself, but had no time to reflect. I was immediately asked "*Have you anything to say?*"

Panic-stricken and without pausing for thought, I answered, "*The water's cold. In the basins. That I have to use for shaving. SIR!*"

This amused the officer and the others present. They sniggered, laughing at me and mocking me. I was humiliated. My punishment was extra guard duty which meant polishing up my kit and acting as sentry at the gates one night, which was tiresome but not too onerous a task, but I shall never forget the shame of that occasion.

Throughout my days at Colchester, I was not only bewildered and confused;

I was thoroughly frightened as I was chased here, there and everywhere. I hated with a deep loathing every moment of those four months. How time drags when one is at one's most miserable; my period as a private soldier seemed to last a full twelve months.

In the evenings everyone in my platoon resorted to the NAAFI, situated a few yards beyond the barrack gates; and it became a haven to which we used to retreat after the day's work was over. We could buy a simple evening meal there and relax in an armchair. The tea was made with proper milk, and there was plenty of beer available. They had a ping-pong table, a billiard room and a "quiet room" where one could sit down in comparative peace. I played ping-pong on my first evening at Colchester and billiards the next evening, and began to shed the horrors of the day as a recruit.

The six of us from public schools found it easy to talk to each other. So inevitably we gravitated together, and formed what we called among ourselves the "English Speaking Union". We knew this was arrogant of us, but we were past caring. It was natural that we should sit together in the cookhouse, polish our boots together, and meet after a day's drill in the Quiet Room of the NAAFI, extracting such humour as we could find from the day's experiences. For a couple of days after receiving the TAB injection, we gathered to compare notes and laughed at each other's efforts to drink tea with stiff arms. When fully recovered, we bought platefuls of sausages and mash, and pocketed many bars of milk chocolate. We drank beer and played billiards together; we laughed at the mysterious and fairly nasty cookhouse food; we even found humour in the way the sergeant major swore at us, and we grumbled to each other about our efforts to keep our kits everlastingly clean. We cheered each other up with shared misery and generally returned to the barracks most evenings in a more relaxed frame of mind.

There was some respite. On the first and second Saturdays at the camp and on some subsequent weekends, we were free after a 12.30pm rifle inspection. If we passed it, we were allowed to slip away. I was able to jump on a train to London and go up to Hampstead to reach Margaret and Roger's[1] little house or Peaks'[2] flat for a late lunch. I could then go down to St Pancras for the train

---

1   My sister, Margaret had married Roger Little in 1950 and bought a small house in Willow Road in Hampstead.

2   'Peaks' was the family's name for my elder sister, otherwise known as 'Liz' who was also living

to Luton to spend a night with my parents and all the comforts of Brooke House[3]. I did nothing much during those precious peaceful family weekends but collapse in an easy chair, read a magazine or two, write a few letters, and perhaps go for a stroll with my father to gather strength for the coming week. On the first Sunday morning out of the barracks, I slept in my own bed at home until lunchtime - which I have never done before or since.

The only other occasion on which I escaped the camp was in November when I was called to attend a WOSB at Barton Stacey near Andover. This was the War Office Selection Board to which one applied for promotion to become an officer; it was a strange affair. Over three days, candidates were put through a series of written intelligence tests, and lots of general knowledge questions. Then we were divided up into small groups and given practical exercises out of doors. For example, each group was given three empty oil drums and a couple of planks of wood and told to get themselves and the drums across a stream. These were tests of common sense, team spirit, management ability and leadership qualities. We were all too worried about passing to enjoy the challenge; and by no means everyone got through. I was very anxious on my return to Colchester, and immensely relieved when their decision reached me in the form of a letter certifying that I was selected for training as an Officer Cadet.

Eaton Hall, Chester

Officer Cadets were trained in three places at that time. Professional soldiers attended the Royal Military Academy at Sandhurst; gunners, that is potential artillery officers trained at Woolwich, and National Service officers for nearly all other arms went to Eaton Hall, near Chester. So I was destined to spend four months at Eaton Hall in order to become an officer in the British Army.

Sometime in early December 1950, my kitbag stuffed with my army clothing and equipment, and the latest Dornford Yates in my pocket, I caught a train from Euston for the long journey to Chester. There I scrambled on to an army truck collecting new arrivals, was taken out to Eaton Hall, and began my new life as an Officer Cadet.

My companions on the course could not have been more different from

---

in Hampstead while working in the West End.
3   Brooke House had been our family home on Hart Hill in Luton since 1937.

those with whom I had lived and worked at Colchester. My fellow officer cadets came from a variety of backgrounds, but most had come straight from school like me. Many had charm and good humour and all seemed to be easy and pleasant people to work with. Mike Casey from Colchester was there; a good fellow named Ben Lewers was in my hut and became a close colleague later. Some were tough and active men from the good grammar schools in the North of England; others came from wealthy homes via Eton and Winchester and were destined for the best cavalry and guards regiments for their commissioned service. I was thrown together with two Old Etonians named Drysdale and Carver, and a Wykehamist named Ellis whose company I much enjoyed.

We still wore the uniform of a private soldier, except that we had two white tabs on our lapels and a white lanyard round our left shoulder. We were still required to obey implicitly the orders of corporals, sergeants, and the RSM, addressing them as *"Staff!"* and they addressed us as *"Sir!"* or *"Gentlemen!"* both on and off parade. We came much more directly under the instruction of officers at the rank of Captain and above. My platoon was under the command of Captain Scott MacDonald of the Black Watch with a strange accent from north of the Border, often seen wearing a very fine kilt, who subsequently served in Korea. Our Company Commander was another Scot with years of experience and a bluff, hearty and thoroughly laid-back demeanour.

The Hall itself was a huge Gothic pile - there is no other word for it - built and occupied before the war by the Duke of Westminster. The officer cadets saw very little of its interior apart from the entrance hall and one or two big downstairs rooms where we messed. The management and training staff lived there and were, I imagine, very comfortable. On the left hand side of the Hall facing it were extensive stables and offices surrounding a rather dark and dank cobbled courtyard where we did drill under the RSM. Under his keen eye and thunderous voice, we had to keep alert, as never before; our boots on the cobbles made a satisfying noise and happily I was generally able to keep up and perform there without further censure.

On arrival we were allocated to a platoon and a Nissen Hut where we were accommodated for the duration of the course. Most were set in lines on the right hand side of the entrance drive looking across at the Hall itself and its forecourt which contained a circular pond with a fountain in the middle. The huts had no permanent heating, and were warmed by huge iron stoves, placed centrally with pipes going up through the roof and requiring to be fed constantly with fuel. That winter was very cold with snow on the ground both before and after the Christmas break, and care of the stove in the huts became everyone's principal concern. Each morning, the first person to wake up had to leap out of bed and light the stove - and then cosset and coddle it until it crept into life and began to warm the room. Meanwhile the rest of us cowered under our blankets with ice on the inside of the windows and snow blowing in through holes in the corrugated iron roof.

Somebody always switched on the wireless full blast at the unearthly hour at which we were woken and we rose from our beds and dressed each morning to the same grating tunes. Several were repeated over and over again and were popular in those days, but had no musical merit and unsurprisingly have not stood the test of time. I still shudder when I remember the painful songs like *"Goodnight Irene, I'll see you in my dreams,"* and *"put another nickel on the nickelodeon."*

The aim of the training was to teach us to be officers in the British army and was subtly different from the basic training we had done ourselves. We still had to do a great deal of boot-polishing and rifle drill, to dress smartly and appear impeccable on parade, but the marching and saluting were balanced with lectures on military topics - administration and organisation - the army loved paperwork in those days. We also went on numerous "schemes"; that is tactical exercises on the ground, learning how to dig in and defend a location or to deploy to attack the enemy, whether in small ten-man sections, platoons of forty men, or companies of three or four platoons. We were required to keep fit with regular PT, route marches and runs. We dug trenches endlessly, did night exercises, and had frequently to tackle the long and hair-raising assault courses in the grounds. I never enjoyed them because I was always drenched and covered in mud, harried and hustled all the way, falling off the walls, tumbling in the water, and scrambling over the massive obstacles.

For recreation we had the opportunity at weekends to go into Chester on the bus, spend 1/9d at the cinema or have drink or two at a pub. Blossoms in the main street was expensive but comfortable; another hostelry on the opposite side of the road was more reasonable in price. After a Saturday evening quenching our thirst at the pub, we sometimes came back to camp on the top of a double-decker bus making a lot of noise singing the customary army marching songs like *"Tipperary"*. The bus driver used to be very angry with us, though I do not think my platoon ever did any damage to his vehicle; and we had to sober up on approaching the guard room at the main gates.

Eaton Hall was too far away for me to get home for a night at the weekend after the customary Saturday morning inspection. On one Bank Holiday in the spring, however, Drysdale was going down south in his big black car - I think it was a Riley - and took me with him for some particular party he had organised. His vehicle was heavy and cumbersome with a long bonnet; after an hour or so, he gave me the wheel while he shut his eyes in the passenger seat. We were on the A41, a long straight two-lane highway running through Shropshire, and I was driving what was then considered fast - probably around 60 miles an hour. To my horror I touched another car coming equally fast in the other direction on the crown of the road; our hub caps kissed as we past each other at speed. There was a lot of noise but after careful inspection by the roadside we found no damage to either vehicle. I was lucky - but Drysdale did not trust me to drive any more and took back the steering wheel for the remainder of the journey.

Our platoon went out on to military training grounds for week-long exercises on two occasions. Shortly before Christmas in very cold weather, we found ourselves digging in on rugged hills behind a place aptly called Mold. We were in the rugged Welsh Marches only a stone's throw from Chester, in wilder and rougher country than I knew in the south of England. Required to live in our trenches and sleep in them for several nights, we were wet and cold in sodden clothes most of the time. None of us could say we enjoyed the experience but we had our first taste of life 'in the field' and were satisfied with our performance when we returned to camp.

On the second major exercise in early March we were taken down to Okehampton on Dartmoor and had the run of the extensive military ranges there. Once again it was cold and wet. We were accommodated for part of the time in one of the half dozen huts of a small permanent camp above the market town. We were well cared for and fed there, but on the moors we went through treacherous bogs in the valleys, and were blanketed by swirling mist on the tors. We dug our trenches through a thin covering of snow, cowered in them for shelter from the freezing wind, and slept in them huddled in our great coat and blankets. When the weather cleared, we made our attack on a position which the 'enemy' defended firing live rounds over our heads - which was yet another new and unwelcome experience.

Soon after Easter 1951 we took our places in a Passing Out Parade in front of the Commandant and senior officers, and attended a solemn and beautiful farewell service in Eaton Hall Chapel. We sang John Bunyan's hymn, then *"Jerusalem"*, and three other hymns during a long service; and the Chaplain closed with the OCTU prayer and this dedication.

> *"O ALMIGHTY GOD, Father of our Lord Jesus Christ, we dedicate to thee this day the years that lie before us. Grant that we may serve our fellow men with zeal and sincerity. And grant that we may uphold that which is right and true, and strengthened by thy Power we may always defend the freedom of our land and the rights of our people. Give us a strong faith, a keen hope and an earnest desire always to follow in the steps of Our Lord Jesus Christ, and to serve thee faithfully all the days of our lives. Amen."*

We were given the opportunity to state our preference of Regiment in which we would like to serve as junior officers. I asked for the Dorset Regiment. If I had wanted to be stationed within easy reach of home, I should have asked to join the Bedfs and Herts Regiment but reports of it at that time were not encouraging; I might equally have opted for the Essex Regiment, except that I cordially loathed it for my treatment as a recruit. I decided to go for the Dorsets both because I loved the county where I had enjoyed five good years at school, and because their 1st Battalion was then stationed in Vienna. The Dorsets were a part of the British military presence in the Quadripartite Occupation Force, working with our three allies and keeping a close eye on the aggressive Red Army there; and I thought it would be both exciting and enjoyable to be a member of their officers' mess.

Plumer Barracks

I received my Commission on 22nd March 1951, and was paid 13/= a day less 4d, rising to 17/6d daily, with 6d tax a year later. I was commissioned into the Dorset Regiment as requested, but never got anywhere near Austria. Instead in the middle of 1951, I was posted as a Second Lieutenant to the Wessex Group

April 1951. Plymouth. Second Lieutenant in the Dorsetshire Regiment - pleased with myself.

Training Centre at Plumer Barracks on Crownhill, north of Plymouth. I was to become a Platoon Commander and a Training Officer in charge of a platoon of new recruits - such as I had been myself only a few short months previously. The tables were turned.

Each platoon consisted of three sections of eight or ten National Servicemen aged eighteen or nineteen, led by a corporal who reported to a sergeant who reported to me as 'his' officer. Most of my dealings were thus with the Sergeant who was a Regular soldier, was a good deal older than me, and knew a lot more than me about young men and about soldiering too. Sergeants Pugsley and Creech with whom I worked for most of the time at Crownhill were tough and reliable men who had seen some years' service in the ranks; they were good with the young men in their charge and generally able to get the best out of them. Despite their knowledge and skill, it was I who was responsible for the conduct of the Platoon, as is the Army's way, reporting for most purposes to the Company Commander, who generally held the rank of Major of many years seniority. Many of those under whom I served then and later had a vast experience of the soldier's craft, having fought either in the Far East against the Japanese or in France after D Day where the Wessex Division had distinguished itself on many occasions.

Plumer Barracks was like all the others - a row of ugly brick-built barrack blocks in which lived the unfortunate recruits, in front of a large area of macadam on which parades took place, and opposite a row of offices and messes. My home was the Officers' Mess which was a comfortable house beside the road that ran from the village of Crownhill out into the country. The Mess was of the standard design; on the left of the entrance was the ante-room with comfortable armchairs, scattered newspapers, and lots of occasional tables. We gathered there for a drink before dinner and relaxation whenever off duty. Beyond the ante-room was the bar presided over by the President of the Mess Committee (PMC) to whom reported the Mess Sergeant; and opposite was our dining room, staffed by young mess waiters. Our sleeping quarters were along a corridor to the right of the front door and in an annex beyond the main building.

My mess bill was started at about £5 a month and rose later to around £7. My monthly pay and allowances amounted to £19:3/=, and my father gave me an additional allowance of £5 so my monthly income was just £24 of which the mess bill took a large slice. I had few other expenses however; I subscribed to World Books in order to have something to read and I paid 10/6d twice a year to remain a member of the Ace of Clubs to keep in touch with my Luton friends.

My bedroom looked through shrubs on to the main road and was little more than a box with room for bed, chest of drawers, desk, wardrobe for my uniforms and a couple of chairs. It was difficult to turn round in such a cluttered space but perfectly adequate for a young bachelor. A batman was allocated to me on arrival who had to make my bed and clean and polish my boots and kit as well as his own. He did a good job; I never remember having to concern myself with my turn-out thereafter.

My uniform was the conventional officer's Service Dress held in place with a Sam Browne belt (that took a lot of polishing), khaki shirt and tie, and just one pip on each shoulder. I wore the cap badge of the Dorset regiment - the castle and key superscribed *"Gibraltar"*, and on my lapels were sewn their sphinx superscribed with the word *"Marabout"*. I managed to look quite smart and reasonably well turned-out when occasion demanded. I had also to purchase "blues" (No. 1 Dress), with the sphinx badge on the collar, for wear on special occasions in the evenings, and I had to borrow a sword to wear on the Battalion parades on the Square. Back home in Luton, I proudly wore this uniform once or twice and was mortified when my schoolboy friend, Hugh Clark, called me a "*one-pip wonder*".

The Crownhill Mess comprised two or three unmarried Captains and Majors, and eight or so subalterns around my age or perhaps a couple of years older, hailing from the various county regiments of the South West of England. We were all bachelors and lived in the Mess; while the older married men lived in married quarters scattered around the northern outskirts of Plymouth; they might have a drink with us after work, but dined in the Mess only occasionally on Mess Nights. We were all new to each other and for one reason or another it was a dull Mess.

Among my contemporaries were however some very pleasant men. Edward-Collins hailed from the Devonshire Regiment and was unusual in that he was Regular, and went on to have a distinguished army career. Mike Cobbold was a Wiltshire and later turned up in Hong Kong. John Webber was a Dorset like me, nearing the end of his National Service. Ben Lewers had been at Eaton Hall with me, joined the Devonshire Regiment and had a platoon at Crownhill alongside mine. David Wynne-Griffiths was a Devon with his home at Churston Ferrers, and John Dudley was another Devon. David Barlow had a large motor cycle and used to roar over Rowborough Down (then unfenced) at 70 miles an hour. Our Company Commander was Captain 'Darts' Dartnall who had won an M.C. at Arnhem; Major Roly Hill was Second in Command of the Training Centre; Lieutenant Colonel Douglas Gaye was the CO of the Training Centre and ran a tight ship - as it were - with quiet efficiency. I liked him; he was somewhat remote from his junior officers but he kept a friendly eye on us and saw that we did nothing stupid while we got the work done. He left the Army after the end of this tour of duty and to my surprise went to Cambridge to take holy orders where I met him again.

At the barracks were some eight platoons at various stages of Basic and Continuation Training. The Basic Training lasted seven weeks and was no different from what I had been put through myself the previous year - rifle drill, rifle care, use of the Bren gun and Sten gun, bayonet practice, field craft and training schemes, camouflage and personal concealment, physical exercises and assault courses, and route marches and cross-country running. Time was also set aside for 'education', 'Padre', health lectures, and film shows. The poor recruits also had to have the TAB injections and vaccinations that were in those days so painful.

The Continuation Training was more of the same. We had Dartmoor on our doorstep and the Willsworthy Ranges a few miles to the north of us, so we were able to exercise there whenever we liked in all weathers. The moor remained an inhospitable place and I frequently took recruits up in foul weather to struggle through marshes and very rough ground, and over streams and rocky hilltops in the course of an attack on a mythical enemy; generally they enjoyed the challenge but occasionally it was simply too wet to be any fun at all.

Our rifle range was at Antony across the Tamar. Every Thursday morning we piled into three-ton trucks and were driven down to the ferry to Torpoint, into Cornwall and across a spit of land to a site looking out over the English Channel. We assembled at the rifle butts with our backs to some cliffs and fired over a stretch of flat ground out to sea where our bullets spent themselves harmlessly in the waves. I always enjoyed the ranges though constantly a little worried about the risk of a recruit firing in the wrong direction. In fine weather it was a supremely beautiful spot and an idyllic place for a picnic, but the noise of the soldiers' shooting for three or four hours on each visit was shattering. We, the instructors, spent one full day a week there for perhaps thirty weeks that year - the Quartermaster calculated the recruits fired well over 1,000,000 rounds of .303 on those ranges; and only much later were we aware of the damage such intensive firing did to our hearing.

We were training young men to serve in various tight spots across the world, so the training was for real. We were aware that the skills that the soldiers learnt from us would help them as they fought the Communist guerrillas in the Malayan jungle or the Chinese hordes in the hills and paddy fields of Korea. In late April 1951, not long after I received my Commission, the men of The Glosters of the Commonwealth Division in Korea had fought for their lives at the Battle of the Imjin River - and sadly there had been many casualties. To the best of our limited abilities, we wanted our recruits to absorb from our teaching as much as fast as they could before they left the country whether on active service or other duties. Through our hands went nearly 3,000 National Servicemen and 200 Regular soldiers, of whom 1,250 ended up in Korea, and another 1,000 in other theatres.

We worked the soldiers on Saturday mornings and might require them to attend a Church Parade every now and then, but otherwise Saturdays and Sundays were at leisure. Ben and I went down to Plymouth by bus one day in April and bought identical light-weight motor cycles. They were James "Cadets", of a mere 122 cc, very easy to drive though slow and noisy. The price was £105 for which I cashed a National Savings Certificate. This purchase greatly expanded our horizons and our weekend pleasure; over the period I ran this little machine, I covered about 250 miles a month and was able to nip down to Plymouth regularly.

The town was in a sad mess. South of Mutley Plain the city and harbour had been laid waste by German bombs ten years previously, and one drove through many acres of devastation around the skeleton of Charles Church to reach the Hoe. Rebuilding had started by the time of my arrival; Royal Parade, Armada Way and New George Street had been laid out, a giant Woolworths was open at one end of the Royal Parade and the old departmental store called Dingles was shortly to reopen at the other end, with a couple of chemists and a shoe shop in a new line of shops in its lee. Otherwise the area that was to become the busy shopping centre was a forest of steel frames rising from the old town's ashes. There were very few cars about this desolate scene - most people travelled by bus.

Union Street had been terribly knocked about, but a dilapidated old cinema had survived and a scruffy theatre flourished under the patronage of the sailors from naval ships in the port. It was something of a red-light district. Several of us from the Mess went one night for a bit of fun to an old-fashioned music hall there. It was noisy and crude; the audience was very rough, and many were drunk. It was an experience that we did not repeat.

I was also able to explore parts of Devon on my trusted motor-cycle. I went on several occasions to Yelverton where one of my fellow officers invited me to play tennis on a grass court of a country house belonging to his parents. Ben and I sometimes went further afield and put our little bikes to the steep hills leading up to Princetown and beyond. We used to make Two Bridges our destination for a pint and a stroll on a summer Saturday evening, and would gather there with several of our fellow subalterns who motored out by car. One chap had a very smart but unreliable bright red MG coupe which was fun to drive but did not always go when one pressed the starter. Once I set off on my own on foot behind the Two Bridges Hotel for a scramble and toiled up beside a stream tumbling down the hill to the road; I drank the clear cool water from it as it was a warm afternoon, but was shaken to come upon a dead pony in the water a hundred yards higher up. Dartmoor was our playground as well as our training area for my six months at Plumer Barracks.

I had one spell of leave over this period. I spent it on the Norfolk Broads with a couple of fellow subalterns. It was an inexpensive way to escape completely the rigours of army life and did me much good.

The Dorset Depot, Dorchester

The Training Centre was closed down in December 1951. I had expected to complete my service there, but the powers that be had decided that Basic Training should in future be done at the Regimental Depots. Plumer Barracks was subsequently demolished and replaced by an office block for civil servants; and in January 1952, I was posted to the Dorchester Depot to carry on doing the same job as before, but in a rather different location. I jumped on my noisy little motor cycle and rode over from Plymouth ready to start all over again.

The Dorchester Officers' Mess was of the standard design with a pleasant ante-room, bar and dining room on the left of the front door, as well as perhaps a dozen single bedrooms along corridors in the ground and first floors. In contrast to Crownhill, however, I was the only subaltern living in for much of my time at Dorchester. John Webber was transferred from Crownhill too, but he disappeared back into civilian life before long. The CO of the Depot was Major Dennis Worrall who was close to retirement and owned a big house some way out of the town. 'Darts' Dartnall came over from Plymouth and became the Training Officer and my immediate superior, and he too lived out with his family; Tim Ealand was a senior Lieutenant and our Adjutant when I arrived, and newly married to Anne. Captain Steve Elvery was a bachelor and lived in, while doing the job of Adjutant of the 4th Battalion which was the Regiment's

Territorial Army unit based at the Depot. For a while, therefore, Steve and I were the only residents at the mess.

The mess was never dull, however; while the Battalion was in Vienna, the Depot was the home base, and Dorset officers used to call in for a night or two on their way to other duties or to Vienna. Better still, the part-time TA officers used the Mess as a sort of club-house; Jimmy Foot who commanded HQ Company of the 4th Battalion and had dealings with the local brewery was always in and out and made sure we were stocked up with good bitter. The bar was often busy and full of cheerful men enjoying a pint after a day's military exercise before returning to their homes. My mess bill went up in such convivial company and was frequently in excess of £8 a month.

The first intake of recruits to the Depot arrived on 17th January in a snow storm. They were very different in character from the mixed bag we had trained at Plymouth; the men who joined up at Dorchester were drawn from the villages and little towns of the county, were slower and quieter than those I had known before, but often seemed to be stronger in character and firmer in purpose; and I liked working with them. They were split into two platoons. I had *"Plassey"* under Sergeant Pugsley, and Webber had *"Garris"* with Sergeant Creech. We had six weeks to knock the men into shape - that is to give them a basic understanding of life as a foot soldier. It was more intensive training than I had known previously and harder work, but more individual within a smaller and friendlier environment. We kept strict discipline because the Dorset soldier likes his pint, but the new men rapidly grew fit with our frequent PT, cross-country running and route marches; they learned drill quickly, and they enjoyed - as I did - rifle shooting both in Poundbury behind the Depot and out on the Sydling and Chickerell ranges near Weymouth. We also encouraged sport; I had to organise and run masses of games, and on free afternoons I found myself playing hockey again with the men, and even football on a pitch at the back of the barracks. I became interested in the work and grew more involved and began to relish the responsibility. It was there that I started to enjoy soldiering and feel I was being useful and perhaps making a positive contribution.

Soon after the arrival of our first intake of new recruits, King George VI died. The nation went into mourning; the Mess wireless relayed solemn music all day; the papers carried photographs of the royal womenfolk shrouded in black; all social functions were postponed, including the Regiment's 250th anniversary celebrations; and the officers put on black arm-bands and black ties. A special church parade was held on the Sunday following the King's death, and on 15th February the two training platoons put on their best battledress and marched out to witness the reading of the proclamation of Queen Elizabeth II by the Deputy High Sheriff. I marched down in front of one platoon and Webber led the other, with Major Worrall at our head. The dignitaries stood on a dais in front of the St Peter's Church in Dorchester town centre amid a big crowd of well-wishers, and we all gave three cheers for Her Majesty. It was a unique and sad occasion for us all. Our trainees look surprisingly smart, given that they had been soldiers for only a few weeks; I was the one who was out of order in that my sock suspender broke while marching back in front of my platoon up the hill to the Keep.

Those young men had their passing out parade at the end of February and were posted to join the 1st Battalion in its final months at Vienna. The second intake arrived in mid March and passed out in early May, ready for Vienna; and the third intake followed on their heels. We also offered Continuation Training for soldiers in their second and third months at the depot. The training became routine but to me the more stimulating and challenging as I began to understand what I was doing. I started to learn more about the individual men in my charge, their backgrounds, interests and aspirations. The job became rewarding.

On the social side, there was always something going on with the TA's friendly officers. In late April, they converted our gymnasium into a passable ball-room for the local Hunt and the TA officers to hold the South Dorset 'Point-to-Point Ball'. Steve and I, the two bachelors in the Depot Mess, were invited and provided with partners; we dressed up - I wore my Blues and felt quite smart, and we shared a table with two other couples whom we knew well, and were given a very good time. I wrote home merrily,

> *"We had dinner at the King's Arms and then came on here. The gym was really well decorated - masses and masses of flowers which made all the difference, and huge coloured parachutes covering the wall-bars. There was a good band and a first-rate bar in the balcony upstairs, another in the Mess and a buffet in the Mess. They put the*

prices up for the night but we decided it would be cheaper in the long run to have champagne - and very good it was too. Numbers were just right - only a hundred and fifty though the tables all round the wall, the band, the flowers and greenery gave the impression that the room was well filled. I came away with the sense of a very enjoyable evening."

A similar successful regimental dance took place in the gym on 28th May, and gave me a particularly happy birthday. Immediately after that dance, Steve in his capacity as TA Adjutant invited me to join him on an exercise in the Bovington Training Area. The weather was very hot on the wild sandy heath. Camouflaged among the heather our role was to defend Gallows Hill from an attack by two TA Companies. I wrote home,

"The TA Captain and I were supposed to represent half the enemy the Companies were to attack. The other half was two carriers and their drivers. We had a wonderful time. We rushed about in these carriers all over the hills, fired a variety of weapons, defended a position to the last man, then - it being an exercise - we withdrew successfully, counter-attacked and were driven off, and finally came up as a tank until their anti-tank gun theoretically knocked us out."

The Editor of the Regimental Journal was kind enough to say:

"Thanks must go to 2/Lieut Eberlie of the Depot staff who turned out to help the Adjutant as enemy, putting up the usual smoke screen, firing brens into pits, and just managing to escape the legitimate attentions of a rather weary D Company, plodding onwards through a valley of thunder flashes, denoting DF fire."

I was very glad I had been persuaded into doing it; it was the sort of soldiering I liked - entirely voluntary but somehow quite satisfying.

Basic training remained our *raison d'etre,* but the third intake and their officers had time off in order to witness the Queen's visit to the Depot. After just four months on the throne, she paid us a call. She couldn't stay to lunch but arranged to spend most of one morning with us. We knew she was coming long before the big day because the barracks were smartened up, and the Officers' Mess was completely redecorated; two of the bachelor bedrooms - one of them mine - were converted into her withdrawing room. On 5th July, escorted by Major-General

G. N. Wood, the Colonel of the Regiment, she visited the Museum in the Keep, inspected a Guard of Honour provided by the TA Battalion, and took a glass of sherry in our Mess where senior officers and their wives were presented to her. I played my part in the smartening the place up, but was otherwise a spectator that day, though impressed by the bearing not only of the young queen but also of the old soldiers who formed the Guard of Honour. It was a good day for the Regiment.

The next event was the return of the 1st Battalion from Austria. They were sent to a temporary camp on Salisbury Plain and disappeared on leave, but not before several officers had called at the Depot and given me a flavour of their life. Word came round that they were destined for Hong Kong in the autumn; and, as I was enjoying myself, I decided to extend my army service by a third year in order to accompany the battalion on their Far East posting. I consulted my father who bravely agreed, while keeping to himself the knowledge that my decision would postpone for yet one more year his opportunity to retire from full-time work. I consulted St John's College[4] who agreed to postpone my arrival until October 1953; and I asked the Regiment if I could stay with them a little longer. They seemed happy at the prospect. As the Regimental Journal has it - rather unkindly, *"2/Lieut Dick Eberlie decided to forsake Cambridge for a while and hastily signed on for another year so that he could have a 'holiday' in Hong Kong at the Government's expense."*

The sixth intake found itself heavily involved in the Regiment's 250th Anniversary Celebrations. We were all swept up in the Tattoo that took place over three evenings at the end of August. We had to do our normal work to ensure the troops went through the full training programme to be ready to join the 1st Battalion. At the same time, they were asked to put on old uniforms, perform antiquated drills and present tableaux about various incidents in the Regiment's distinguished history since its formation early in the eighteenth century. The organiser was Colonel Geoffrey White, whom we all knew as Knocker - why I do not know - and who was later to take charge in Hong Kong. He had a powerful presence and bags of drive, won the DSO commanding the Battalion after Kohima in Assam where, in some of the toughest fighting of the

---

4 I had won a place at St John's College, Cambridge, shortly before leaving school in early 1950, and the College had agreed to keep this place open for me while doing my National Service.

war, the British army had held the Japanese advance and turned the tide of the campaign. Knocker was a great showman and the Tattoo was his triumph. He required the new recruits to fight the Battle of Plassey, cross the river Rhine at Arnhem, and man the burning troopship, the Sarah Sands with her sails and quarter deck on fire in the middle of the Indian Ocean. My particular role was to make sure she burned satisfactorily each night. It was said shortly after the event, "*The recruits of the Basic Platoon are more than anyone else the heroes of the Tattoo.*" This was my platoon and I was proud of them - young Private Rawlings who helped me rebuild Sarah Sands every night after she was destroyed by fire was rapidly promoted to sergeant.

There was of course much else in the way of Guards of Honour, Massed Bands beating Retreat, PT Displays, Drill Displays, and an Artillery Drive by the Dorset Yeomanry. The 1st Battalion joined in the party, marching through the county town with bayonets fixed and with great panache, holding another big dance in the gym, and running a Regimental Cricket Week on the lovely ground on the Weymouth Road, while the band and drums performed on numerous occasions both in the town and at the barracks. One of the happiest occasions was a summer evening cocktail party thrown by our CO, and his wife at their beautiful home deep in the Dorset countryside. The butler handed us White Ladies which was a delicious concoction with beaten egg white floating on top but was the devil to drink!

The tattoo and accompanying parties closed my service at the Depot in triumph. Since January I had seen six intakes, comprising around 400 men, through their Basic training. I had enjoyed a little responsibility and lots of fun, and I was hugely looking forward to leading my own platoon of trained men as an integral part of the Battalion overseas.

Socially, I was fortunate in having contacts around the county, travelling always on my faithful motor bike. I went back to Sherborne on several occasions to help in training young cadets, testing them on their fieldcraft and advising on aspects of their training. I was invited over in July to accompany a group of American girls on a tour of the West Country after a high old time in London. We took them in a variety of cars to see the sights of Dorset, starting with Cerne Abbas and the Giant, driving on to Studland Bay, picnicking and swimming at Lulworth Cove, looking at old Corfe Castle, and ending with a noisy party back at Sherborne.

I was a guest of the Ross-Skinners[5] from time to time. I went with them once to watch exhibition tennis matches by the champions of the day, Hoad, Rosewall and others, on the Radipole Courts at Weymouth; another time they took me to a show at the little theatre there and finished the evening eating fish and chips out of newspapers on the front. On the way to a black tie event at Warmwell one dark evening, I slid off my bike taking a steep bend too sharply, made a mess of my suit and arrived hot, embarrassed and dirty, but nevertheless managed to enjoy myself meeting their guests.

The family came down to the South West too. I chuntered down for a long weekend in late May to join Margaret and Roger, and Roger's sister, Anne[6] on holiday in a caravan in an empty field looking out to sea near St Mawes. The view was superb, but I had to sleep on sodden ground; the weather was poor and, while I always enjoyed my sister's company and delicious meals, it was too wet to be much fun. I spent a weekend in July with my parents and Liz on holiday staying in great comfort at the Manor House Hotel at Moretonhampstead. In many ways I was sad when life at Dorchester came to an end and I joined the 1st Battalion.

---

5 Colonel and Mrs Ross-Skinner had lived near Luton and as a small boy I had been a close friend of their son Harry John, but he had moved with his parents to Warmwell House near Dorchester after the war.

6 Anne Little was then a nursing sister in an East End Hospital, and unmarried.

Chapter 3

Hong Kong: Soldiering

🍒 🍒 🍒

They send us along where the roads are, but mostly we go where they ain't.

From *Screw-Guns* by Rudyard Kipling

🍒 🍒 🍒

Outward Bound

I was taken on the strength of the 1st Battalion in early September 1952 and reported at Chisledon Camp on Salisbury Plain where they were encamped. I then went off on embarkation leave. I went home for a few days; I had the opportunity to drive my mother over to Aldeburgh to see Grannie Spinks - and sadly it was the last time I saw her, as she died that November while I was abroad. A day or two later my parents and I took the car up to the Lake District for a week at the Prince of Wales Hotel at Grasmere. It was a pretty place with a garden that ran down to the lake, and my father and I used it as a base from which to go for long walks in the rain; we climbed Helvellyn in thick mist, we tackled Striding Edge, explored the hills and lakes, and went over to watch hounds trailing in Langdale. Does one ever really know one's parents? I got to know my father and mother much better then than perhaps at any time previously, and greatly enjoyed their company.

I went back to Chisledon at the end of my leave and joined the Battalion on the train journey down to Southampton docks where we embarked on the troopship, the SS Empire Fowey on 3rd October 1952. We had a happy send-off from the quayside the following morning by the Colonel of the Regiment, the Mayor of Dorchester, any number of Generals and Colonels, lots of Old Comrades, military bands, and families and friends. Few visitors were allowed aboard; so speeches of farewell were made over loudspeakers and we shouted to each other across the narrow strip of water between ship and dockside.

My parents left home at 5.30am to join the throng on the quay, and waited and waved as the ship cast off at midday. There was a lump in my throat as I waved energetically back from a precarious vantage point on the upper deck; and as we slipped down the Solent, I watched them as they grew smaller and smaller until mother's purple coat faded out of sight. Though sad to be leaving my family behind, I was hugely excited at the adventure ahead.

The Dorset Officers

Confinement in a ship for a month was a good way to get to know one's brother officers and their wives. These were the men and women with whom I was to work and play over the coming months.

Tom Affleck-Graves was the Colonel. He was a tall, slim and well-built man who had served with the Dorsets during the war - he had fought with the 2nd Battalion before Dunkirk - and had a distinguished record. He had taken over the Battalion in Vienna and overseen its 250th anniversary celebrations there, but sadly he was not well on this trip. He seemed often to be in pain and under stress both on board and in the early days after arriving in the New Territories. He brought us out to the Far East and welded us together into a single unit but had to take a good deal of time off. Only six weeks after reaching Hong Kong he flew home.

Reggie Hill was a Major and the Second in Command and took over when the Colonel was ill or absent. Reggie's wife, Doris, thus became our 'first lady' and kept a motherly eye on us youngsters. I was frightened of Reggie and do not think he approved of me. He thought I was a poor messing officer and when acting as CO gave me a sharp rocket for failing to salute properly. This hurt because I fancied my salute - but apparently it was not good enough. The RSM agreed with him about me. He said to me one day on the square, *"Mr Eberlie, Sir. I have saluted you twice this morning and you have not had the courtesy to acknowledge me"*. Severely humbled, all I could say in reply was, *"Yes, Mr Webber."*

John Archer was our Adjutant and an affable and friendly man, married to Marie who mixed easily with everyone. John had all the threads in his hands, was terrifyingly efficient and kept us all up to the mark. Charles Wallis was the Assistant Adjutant.

Tony Morris was the Commander of C Company in which I was placed for the voyage, and a charming and most likeable man for whom I found it easy to work. Among many other jobs, Tony later took charge of our forty mules and muleteers at the Camp; and he was one of the privileged few who went home to represent the Regiment at the Coronation Parades in London.

Brian Edwards and Klaus Marx were the other subalterns in C Company; both good athletes, and I later spent many hours in their company training and performing for the battalion athletics team - but how Klaus came by his name I have no idea - it seemed so unlikely.

John Knight was in charge of the Headquarters Company, travelling with his two delightful young sons and his wife Betty. Unhappily she had to be taken off the ship at the South end of the Suez Canal with acute appendicitis, but was able to rejoin us in Hong Kong after a spell in an Egyptian hospital.

Other senior members of HQ Company were John Sims and Bob Feltham in charge of the Battalion's motor transport and a key man. Bob Reep was our Signals Officer, and among many other skills was a first class athlete who led our Athletic Team to victory a little later. John Reynolds had charge of the Antitank Platoon, newly wed to Jocelyn who was very hospitable and kind to me on many occasions;

The HQ Company subalterns were Douglas Jenks, a single man in charge of our Assault Pioneers - the man to turn to when you wanted to blow things up - short and stocky, and a bit of a humourist; and Dick Rowbotham, who was of my vintage, and was transferred to D Company at the same time as I was when we reached our destination. Dick was a very competent chap of the type who must have done well in business later.

John Freer-Smith commanded B Company, and was another charming chap and recently married to Angela, another of the hospitable young wives with a delightful flat in Kowloon. His subalterns were Basil Hebden with some years experience under his belt, and John Gilmore, a younger officer, who had several different jobs and ended up in Brigade HQ. Gerald Blight had a platoon and was a tall man and a fine athlete. He was also both clever (he played in the Colony's Chess Championship) and amusing - indeed he was something of a card and entertained us on many a Dinner Night in the Camp, before he moved out to become the General's ADC.

John Drew was in charge of D Company, married to Maisie, had already served in Korea, and was a delightful boss for whom I was later to work. With him on the boat were two experienced subalterns, Peter Elgar, and John Smoker who had served with the Military Police; both of these two transferred to bigger jobs as soon as we landed in Hong Kong. The one National Service subaltern in D Company at the start was Dick Campbell, whom I was to join in due course.

The very experienced Major Ivor Ramsay led our Support Company and was I think the most senior living-in Mess member. John Wreford, (married to Jo) was a part of his team and later took over a Company. A subaltern in the Company was Ross Moylan who was perhaps the youngest member of the Mess - a laid-back and easy-going type, he drank deeply and was the noisiest of us all when in his cups - and he too moved to D Company on arrival in Hong Kong.

The Officers' mess was completed by the Medical Officer named Peter Boultbee and Padre Dodds, both of whom were pleasant colleagues and good friends to us young single officers.

While some of us were very new to professional soldiering, we were a balanced group led by men who had seen service in the war and with a core of others in their thirties who had eight or ten years service in a variety of peacetime and war-time soldiering. Even though I came straight from the Depot, I was treated from the first day as a full member of the team to which I was proud to belong. With most of these officers I was to work closely and play hard over the following eight months, and I found them likeable and easy to get on with - though none became a close friend. We made up a good mess; and gradually they brought me into the fold and I began to feel part of the Dorset "family".

The SS Empire Fowey

Our ship was reputed to be one of the finest troopships in service and we were comfortable in the First Class, even though four junior officers were required to share each small and airless cabin. The stewards were Lascars who worked hard and looked after us very well; in addition each officer had his own batman so it was an easy life. My batman was a cheerful and sensible lad named Stride. The dining rooms were excellent, and the troops' canteen was of a similar high standard and ran on an American-style cafeteria system that was new to us in England. The troop decks were heavily overcrowded, however, for, in addition to 650 Dorsets of all ranks, there were 900 other passengers - including 250 Royal Fusiliers who came under our wing for the time being. Married officers and NCOs were accompanied by their wives and children, and, while the kids made a racket running around the decks, the ladies provided a civilising and homely influence which I think all the men appreciated.

Each subaltern was responsible for a troop-deck of about 100 soldiers in the deep bowels of the ship. The men in my charge were all Dorsets, but strangers to me, and I spent some time trying to get to know them while organising their messing and sleeping arrangements. After a few days, we slipped into an easy routine on board, and I had merely to check all was well with them each morning during the daily "Ship's Inspection" when the Ship's Commandant came round.

The soldiers' routine on board was soon established. We all turned out for early morning P.T. for twenty minutes from 6.40am. This did us all good and took place at the only time when later in the voyage it was cool enough for us to want to take exercise, but it was a tricky business when the sea was rough and the decks were slippery. After PT, we changed into uniform, and were obliged to sit with rumbling tummies through an hour's "Officers' Lecture" - generally quite interesting but sometimes dead boring. Breakfast was at 9am - there were three sittings of each meal because we shared the big dining room with the children and second class passengers who went through first.

Later in the morning we kept the soldiers occupied with some military training. Space did not allow any running around, but we practised their skills in things like stripping and assembling rifles and Bren guns, and I spent many mornings at the stern of the ship in charge of the "range". Four or five people were able to lie down with rifles firing down the ship's wash where we tossed out empty wooden crates from the galleys. They were tricky targets as they bobbed and bounced from one wave to the next and gradually floated away out of sight. It was rather the same as shooting at bottles at a fairground and was enjoyed by all of us on board. We gave everyone the opportunity of a shoot as long as the supply of old boxes lasted and later sent balloons down the wake for target practice. The soldiers used to queue up for the chance of a shot; the naval ratings and airmen on board tried their hand too; then the army wives were persuaded to have a go and some among them proved excellent shots.

In the afternoons, we changed into civilian clothes - which generally meant an old pair of shorts and shirt - to play deck quoits or deck tennis, or better still sit in a deck chair with a book and a cup of tea, or something stronger. One strenuous activity that I avoided was the tug-of-war competition that lasted most of the four week voyage. As a lightweight, I was not required to pull but was appointed captain of a team of tough young soldiers, and we did well, getting through three rounds, until knocked out in the semi-finals. We then retired to the sidelines to watch the final teams of huge men battle it out.

Officers were required to dress in the evenings. This meant putting on our "blues" while in a temperate climate although changing was not easy for four men trying to dress at the same time in our small cabin, but we had to do it. After dinner, we sometimes had a cigarette and a drink, and chatted in the smoking room, listening to a Singapore-bound Royal Marine Orchestra playing in the background. Some evenings, we were shown a film or had a round of housey-housey. There were occasional dances and musical evenings; and more frequently I found myself playing liar dice or bridge with my fellow subalterns. One's last walk round the deck was delightful when the weather was fair; everything was quiet; the lights shone on the water; the atmosphere was warm and peaceful.

The voyage started slowly in every respect, as it took a few days to get sorted out while we ran into fog down the English Channel and through the Bay of Biscay. The ship crawled forward, at one moment through the middle of a Portuguese fishing fleet, while the fog horn hooted and rumbled like an unhappy cow at regular intervals night and day. It murdered sleep, but at least the sea was smooth until we entered the Mediterranean.

We slipped past Gibraltar without pausing. North of Malta we changed out of battledress into tropical kit on what was supposed to be the start of the hot weather but happened to be the coldest day of the voyage. We thereafter wore green cotton shirts with our pips on the shoulders, khaki shorts held in with a smart belt, and green stockings and boots in the morning, and tennis shoes

In tropical kit at the ship's rail.

and no socks in the afternoons. It was a comfortable dress for the most part, until the heat intensified and we shed shirt and stockings whenever we could. At night when it grew warmer, we put on our Blues trousers and wore short monkey jackets or shark-skin dinner jackets over a cummerbund. Approaching the Egyptian coast, however, the wind got up and it rained steadily all the way to Port Said at the mouth of the Suez Canal, our first stop on the route to the Far East.

We were allowed neither to go into the town nor to visit the famous Simon Artz Bazaar on the quayside. Bumboats came alongside and a hectic trade started between soldiers leaning over the ship's railings on the lower decks and salesmen in the bumboats offering bright red fez, plaited hats, mats, stuffed camels and lots of other attractive but nonsense goods. Other salesmen clambered on to the upper decks and chattered away selling the same rubbish at absurd prices. More fun were the gully-gully men who wandered around the deck and practised their magic on us, and for a few dinars produced busy little yellow chicks from our pockets, ears, noses and everywhere else.

We passed through the northern half of the Canal at night, found ourselves in the Great Bitter Lakes at dawn the next morning, where we were besieged once more by bumboats that lashed themselves to our bulwarks and did steady business. British troops were in occupation of the Suez Canal Zone, and as we set off in convoy down the lower half of the Canal, we frequently passed lorry-loads of bare-chested Tommies labouring under the hot sun, repairing bridges, building jetties and the like. Their shoulders were brick red from long exposure to the sun, and it was their cheery custom to yell across the water to us, cruising past and still pale from home, *"Getchernees brahn!"* and *"Get some in!"* to which our men responded, *"When yer goin' abrahd?"* It caused great amusement and was the constant refrain as we completed our journey down to Port Tawfiq at the southern end of the Canal. Here we paused to disembark poor Betty Knight, in some pain with appendix trouble, I believe. Then we sped on down the Red Sea, while the weather grew hotter and hotter.

We called at Aden overnight and cruised on through the Indian Ocean. We saw nothing but sky and sea for the following five days, but the sea was always interesting; flying fish flipped from one wave to another with flickering silver and transparent wings, dolphins bounded along keeping us company for many knots; we saw the occasional shark in the distance; and the skies were a delight both at dawn and at sunset, while at night in cloudless skies the stars seemed huge and very close.

At Colombo, we had our first taste and smell of the East. After the ship had anchored, the passengers were allowed four hours ashore and were able to wander round the city centre. We spent our first rupees on exotic little elephants carved from 'temple wood', and saw for the first time in our lives the cheerful Sinhalese, their rickshaws, snake charmers, banyan trees, and many exotic and exciting plants and people. Half a dozen of us took a taxi to a tiny restaurant called Pilawoos where we experienced a very hot but delicious Ceylon chicken curry. We had time to visit Mount Lavinia Hotel where we inspected a giant, and perhaps rather sad and lonely turtle in a pond on the front lawn. Then, loaded with bananas and coconuts from the local market we returned to the ship. I decided if this was the East, I was going to enjoy it.

The ship approached Singapore a few days later and slipped between the many beautiful islands on either side of the channel into the harbour. Once again we had only a few hours in which to explore the city while a few passengers disembarked and others came aboard for the final run though the South China Sea. It was dark when we went ashore and several parties of officers found their way to a restaurant called The Cockpit where the tables were set under the stars and we dined al fresco beneath tall coconut palm trees. After a good meal and a couple of drinks, we strolled down to the docks, only to be caught in the mother and father of all rain-storms. As the monsoon ditches filled with turbulent water, we pelted along the pier and reached our ship drenched to the skin. Immediately she hoisted anchor and set off for the long run north to our destination.

As she turned out of the Malay Straits, she was obliged to alter course to port to avoid a typhoon that was sweeping up from the Philippines, drowning many local fishermen on the way. For a couple of days, life was uncomfortable on board. The seas grew very rough, the bows rose to a frightening height before dropping like a great stone into the ocean, and the stern gyrated and thudded, while giant waves swept the open deck. PT was out of the question as the ship rolled and heaved, and white-faced soldiers crawled to their bunks. All port-holes and vents were shut to keep the sea out and the stench on the lower decks was most unpleasant. Reggie Hill gave the morning "officers' lecture" on "*The Duties in aid of the Civil Power*" and referred to the use by the Hong Kong Police of "*sick-making gas*"; we subalterns fell about.

I happened to be Orderly Officer that day and was fortunate to be able to keep on my feet. I inspected the troops' canteen and found not a soul in for lunch. Every soldier was in his hammock wishing he were dead...."*a thousand stomachs heaving down below...*" I spent my time going round with Kwells, and assuring everyone it would soon be over. At the same time we were required to prepare for disembarkation; kit had to be packed, clothes to be pressed, equipment cleaned up and Hong Kong dollars issued to each individual for immediate needs, so that the battalion would look smart and be properly equipped on arrival.

On our last evening, John Archer looked me up and invited me into the bar. Now, when the Adjutant offers you a drink, you know he wants you to do something unpleasant. True to form, he told me he wanted me to stay behind when we docked and the battalion disembarked. I was to collect a large sum of

Hong Kong dollars, sort them all out and pay the equivalent of £400 to each of the wives of our soldiers and NCOs before they left the ship. He then added almost as an after-thought that I was appointed Messing Officer for the Officers' Mess in our new Camp. I needed that drink.

It thus transpired that I was running around until late on the night before we docked like the proverbial wet hen and up early in the morning as we approached our destination sorting out money for the families to take ashore. I saw nothing of the ship's approach to Hong Kong Island and Victoria, I missed my breakfast, I neither saw us dock nor heard the massed bands and cheerful ceremony that welcomed us to Kowloon Harbour. I had no chance to wave the battalion off as they marched away to the railway station to board their special train into the New Territories. Instead on a sweltering and sticky lower deck, I was converting pounds into dollars at 1/3d a dollar, and handing out sheaves of notes to many of the soldiers and to a long queue of ladies, many of them with noisy children hanging on their arms.

I then helped the families into the military buses that were to take them to their various hotels, and was able to relax only over lunch on board the deserted boat. I sat with the Baggage Officer who had similarly been detained, and for the first time we were able to admire the view of the great city across the water. We watched the Chinese fishing junks, merchant vessels and naval ships in the great harbour. We were awed by our view of Peak, the funicular railway and all Victoria stretched out along the shore, Government House half way up the hill, and the skyscrapers towering over the water.

The Battalion's baggage was lifted out of the hold and loaded onto a convoy of three ton lorries by Chinese coolies; when all was ready in the late afternoon, I threw my own suitcases into the back of one of the lorries, hitched a lift in its cabin, and off we drove through Kowloon and out into the New Territories.

The New Territories

Kowloon harbour covered a large area; we drove out past extensive wharves, and lines of 'go-downs' where opium must once have been stored in great quantities. On leaving the docks, we saw the Star Ferry that ran across to the Hong Kong Island, the rowdy fish market which smelt powerfully, and the huge edifice of the Peninsula Hotel facing the Island. We then wended our way through the town and up a long hill out into the country.

Our Camp was situated at San Wai on the road half way between the village of Fan Ling and the frontier with China. Two roads ran in those days from Kowloon to Fan Ling each side of the mountainous spine of the peninsula that was the New Territories. One road meandered along the west coast up to the holiday resort of Castle Peak before it cut inland a few miles short of the border. The other road climbed over some tumbling ridges and ran down to the peninsula's east coast through a big fishing village called Taipo and thence also up to Fan Ling. Our convoy decided to take the eastern route which was reported to be of 25 miles, whereas the western road via Castle Peak was said to be 35 miles long.

The journey took an hour and half including a ten minute halt while an overheated engine cooled down and a petrol-feed pipe was repaired. The road was one long procession of W bends. There were no N bends; they were all double or triple turns often on sharp steep corners, and our average speed was around 20 mph. It was exhausting driving; we were told the longer route was

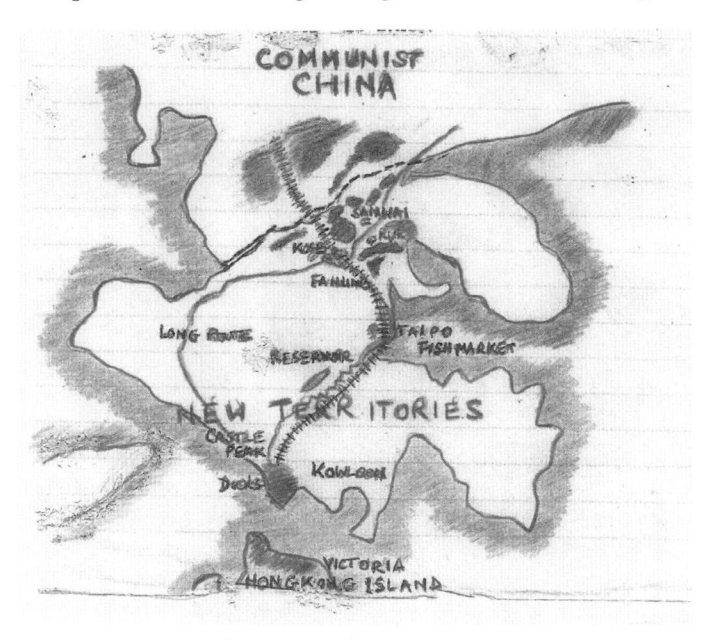

October 1952. The New Territories.

better driving but took much the same time.

I was not impressed with the Chinese villages on our road. The roadside population for the most part lived in shacks. The coastal villages were dependent on fishing and the drying fish stank; the inland villages were surrounded by paddy fields on every pocket of fertile land and on each flat terrace where they scattered human excrement as fertiliser. All the country Chinese were bare-foot and in rags, and most wore huge woven hats as protection from the sun. Some of the women waded knee-deep through the mud and muck behind water buffaloes, planting or weeding their rice shoots. Many of those we saw carried heavy loads on yokes across their shoulders, and some others collected the rice and threshed it by the roadside in wide plaited baskets. On that first journey to our Camp, I thought it all very picturesque, but quite disgustingly smelly. The aroma was all-pervading, and we soon got used to it, but I never found the villages in the least attractive.

As we drove through Taipo on my first journey into the New Territories, I was not encouraged by the view. The inhabitants depended largely on fish which

October 1952. The New Territories. Scratching a living.

they dried on lines strung in the sun which you could smell several miles away. The fishing village was big enough to be an administration centre and have a police station possessing launches for patrolling the coast. There was a passable beach outside the village that we were later to use frequently and a number of cafes and little restaurants along the shore.

At last we came to Fan Ling which we found to be a big village and market at the cross-roads where our road met roads from Castle Peak to the west and China to the north. Fan Ling was our railway station, and the last on the line to China. Brigade Headquarters were sited there in what was euphemistically called Fan Ling Gardens. Two other infantry battalions were close by - the King's Own Scottish Borderers (KOSB) were behind the village, to be replaced in mid November by the Welch Regiment, while the Royal Ulster Rifles (RUR) lay encamped in the valley almost opposite our Camp at San Wai. We three battalions formed the 27th Brigade with an artillery regiment within reach; not far away was the 35th Brigade, comprising battalions of the Royal Norfolk Regiment and the Wiltshire Regiment. The RUR, Welch and Norfolks had all come to Hong Kong after gallant and tough service in the front line in Korea. When later we met their officers and men they never talked of the fighting but wore the medal ribbons on their chests with justifiable pride.

On our first weekend at San Wai, several of my fellow officers and I went out to have a look at the settlement of Castle Peak that lay on the western side of the peninsula, and called on a number of officers' wives and families who had been accommodated in the hotel there straight from the boat on arrival in the Colony. The hotel was modern, shiny and chromium-plated and very convenient, though it offered poor and rather expensive service. It proved unsatisfactory for any length of time, and the families soon moved into Kowloon which offered much better facilities.

A much pleasanter settlement of married quarters and shops in the hills was at Sek Kong, not far off the road to Castle Peak. Here were several very new houses which some of our more senior officers chose for the duration of their tour in the New Territories. The excellent accommodation was situated in congenial surroundings within reach of our Camp. The Drews and the Archers found pleasant bungalows there, although most other married families seemed to prefer Kowloon.

San Wai Camp

Our Camp was a couple of miles up the road from Fan Ling and just one mile from the frontier with China along the eastern coast road. There were hills all round us; two parallel ranges lay between us and the frontier, while immediately behind and above us was Badge Hill where the rocks were embellished with the images of the cap badges of the regiments that had been stationed there over the years. Opposite us in the valley lay the RUR camp whence drifted up in the early morning the shrill sound of bag-pipes, and later in the day the less attractive raucous voice of their RSM. Behind the RUR Camp rose steeply another line of hills; the first was named Birds Hill and the second Cloudy Hill; both rose sharply and climbing them was rough going. Beyond Cloudy Hill lay the Jhelum Valley and on the far side of this valley rose the serious mountains of the Patsin range which almost completely hid a large peninsula of cultivated land that was accessible only by sea.

The Dorset Camp comprised a jumble of Nissen Huts and wooden constructions, many of which were merely glorified shacks, spread out over a gently sloping hillside. The Officers' Mess was newly built on the highest point above terraces on which a semi-circle of huts provided sleeping and living accommodation for the 'living-in' officers.

On three sides below the Mess fanned out the Nissen huts of A, B and C Companies, and behind them lay bigger buildings such as the Sergeants' Mess, the cookhouses, quarters for the Band and Drums, the Battalion Orderly Room which the Adjutant ruled, and numerous other offices. Behind the Mess and over the brow of our hill lay a short rifle range and a makeshift area for throwing grenades.

The lower slopes of the hill were almost cut in half by a stream and bog that was awash in the Rainy Season. Below them were situated D Company lines, the motor transport lines, the mortars and heavier weaponry, while between them and the frontier road lay our parade ground and sports fields which were wide and level and had apparently once been a race track. In the Rains, the stream was full of fat frogs that bellowed all night long in an ecstasy of sexual excitement. I used to enjoy walking back from D Company office to the Mess late in the evening beside the stream with the chorus of the frogs in my ears.

Away to one side were the Mule Lines. We had forty of the beasts on our strength, and they were invaluable in carrying our heavy equipment when we went up into the hills beyond the reach of the jeeps. We were always rude about these poor mules who were as maddeningly stubborn as their name implies and were devilishly difficult to train or lead. We came however to respect their dogged strength as they laboured up the narrow and twisting rocky tracks often high in the mountains to deliver food and bedding, ammunition and weaponry to our dugouts.

Beside the road leading into our Camp were located some very important offices. They were the NAAFI canteen and the shop of the contractor named Au Wai Lam who ran a thriving business as tailor, and sold us a variety of clothing and tropical uniforms. He could knock up two acceptable suits for one over a couple of weeks, charging between 200 and 300 dollars. Down by the tailor was the barber and the dhobi to whom we each paid 22 dollars a month to wash our linen and clothes. Invaluable was his 24 hour service called '*The Flying Dhobi*', which cleaned up our uniforms after our scrambles over the mountains.

Colonel 'Knocker' White

When, shortly before Christmas, Tom Affleck Graves, our original CO, slipped away home by air for treatment for his ulcers, we were told his replacement would be Geoffrey 'Knocker' White. I had worked under him at the Depot where he had organised the 250th Anniversary Tattoo that summer, and I had a huge respect for him - tinged with awe, for I had always found him a heroic and dominating personality. He was totally devoted to the Dorset Regiment and immensely knowledgeable in its history. After running the Tattoo, Knocker had been given a key job in Malaya, but had been only too pleased to give it up in order to rejoin his beloved Regiment. He jumped on the troopship named The Georgic when it called in at Singapore, came up to Hong Kong by sea and landed and took over the Battalion in the middle of January 1953.

I think we all looked forward to his coming to take charge. I was the subaltern in charge of the Guard of Honour for him at the Camp gates on his arrival off the boat. All the officers assembled in the Mess to greet him at lunchtime and gave him a warm welcome. Immediately the atmosphere was very pleasant which was a good augury for the future, and he quickly made his presence felt. He insisted that we honoured the traditions of the regiment and lived up to the high standards that it had set in the past - and he never tired of recalling the glories of the Regiment's battle honours, whether Plassey with Clive in India, or Burma in 1944/45.

Mrs White had stayed at home, so Knocker had his quarters in our Mess and spent many evenings relaxing there among his more junior officers, attending our Dinner Nights and regaling us with his stories of the regiment's past. He often chatted to me, as one of the actors in his tattoo at Dorchester, with his recollections of those triumphant days.

The Dorsets' Job in Hong Kong

During the early morning "Officers' Lectures" on board ship, Tom Affleck-Graves and others explained our role in Hong Kong. Then on the day after our arrival at San Wai Camp, Major General Cruddas, the Army's GOC in the Colony, came to brief us still more fully. Hong Kong had been a British colony for over one hundred years, with a lease from the Chinese that would expire in 1997. Not far to the north of us, they had sent their army into South Korea in hordes only eighteen months before our arrival in the Far East, very nearly destroyed the United Nations forces sent to resist them, and come close to occupying the whole of the country.

We were told we were in Hong Kong to do two things: primarily to deter and prevent a Chinese invasion of the New Territories and Hong Kong Island; and secondly to train reinforcements for the British forces on the front line in Korea. We suspected that the Chinese had no desire to divert troops to do battle with us in the colony; they were far too busy coping with the after-effects of their revolution and managing their heavy commitment in Korea. In any case they were already able to share in Hong Kong's prosperity, and well aware it would drop into their hands as a ripe plum at the end of the lease in a very few years' time. Their government was unpredictable, however, and it seemed prudent to the British colonial power to have defensive arrangements in place. Thus two Brigades with supporting arms were deployed along the frontier between China and the New Territories, and the Dorsets formed one element of 27 Brigade.

The specific tasks of the Dorsets in an "emergency" was to hold any invading force on the line of Birds Hill and Cloudy Hill and to deny the use of the valley below us as a route south to an enemy seeking to reach Hong Kong

Island and the city of Victoria. We were to hold these hills for fourteen days until reinforcements reached us from Singapore. It was reckoned that an attack would come down the valley road rather than over our protective hills, so our predecessors had dug and fortified defensive positions right across the hills from the line of the railway to the sea on the east coast. Privately we may have been uncertain if our small strength could withstand so long the attacks of a vast army such as China was able to deploy. We were all aware of the way in which they had overwhelmed The Glosters at the Imjin River and the well-equipped American forces the previous year, but we kept any doubts to ourselves. We were told we were "operational" from the moment of our arrival in the colony and constantly reminded that the border with mainland China was just one mile north of our Camp. We were given a job to do and our Colonel made sure we would do it as best we could.

D Company

When I arrived in San Wai, I was told I was to move from C Company and given a Platoon in D Company. The Company Commander was John Drew whom I liked and I found myself working with Dick Rowbotham and Ross Moylan, both of whom were congenial colleagues. A third subaltern named Peter Pearmain joined us around Easter.

Just two days after we reached San Wai Camp, the whole Battalion moved up on to Birds Hill for three nights on its first Brigade Manning Exercise in the mountains. A few rough jeep tracks ran about half way up the hills before piles of rocks prevented them going further upwards. Our supplies came up by jeep to this point. Thereafter mules brought up the heavy gear, but most of our equipment was carried on our backs. The hilltops were only 3,000 feet up, but it took two gruelling hours to scramble up the steep rugged hillside to our positions in full kit which included a blanket, groundsheet and mosquito net. D Company positions were on a forward spur of Birds Hill with four strong cement pill-boxes for our Bren guns and a fortified strong-point to our rear (in which I put up my camp bed). We thought it appropriate to call my Platoon headquarters the "*Cuckoo's Nest*" or "*Venomous Villa*" when I found a little snake wrapped round the pole holding up my mosquito net on our first night in residence.

The previous occupants of this defensive site had been the Middlesex Regiment, known as *'The Diehards'*, who were at last going home after tough fighting in Korea that had added many new battle honours to their colours. Up in Birds Hill, their troops had dug a number of deep slit trenches and encircled our position with barbed wire. Wireless communications were good; the only snag was that we had to clamber up a narrow and precipitous track to Company HQ to collect food, water supplies and ammunition.

Our rations were what is known as "Composite" or Compo. They were boxes of thirty tins to feed ten men for a day, and they were first-rate. The tins held sausages, bacon and oatmeal for breakfast, stewed steaks and plum pudding for lunch and supper, with butter, jam, sugar, tea and milk. All one needed in addition was bread and potatoes brought up on the backs of the mules. So we were well fed; and we also carried sufficient water in which to wash and shave in the early morning. Some things went astray, however; we were issued with the wrong ammunition for our rifles which could have been serious; and, even worse, we did not receive our second blankets which were badly needed in the early hours; Cpl Pattenden's section had no blankets at all and we had to scrounge from elsewhere. My bedding-roll eventually arrived on a mule's back, and I passed a reasonable night, though frequently out and about my platoon positions, checking all was well.

With the guidance of the experienced Sgt Brookes, my platoon tried to behave as if a 'live enemy' were present in the valley below us; so we sent out patrols into the jungle below us, put out sentries at night, held our 'stand-to' at dawn and dusk, and arranged constant all-round observation. I took out the patrols after 'stand-to' each evening; Purvis, Lavers and Gordon came with me one night to check the wire below our platoon position and we had a cigarette together afterwards sitting on my bed and chatting about Dorchester and the people we had known at the Depot. I was visited by a little Chinese boy whom we named Chang who attached himself to our Company whenever we were up on Birds Hill. He whittled a stout walking stick for me that I used all the time on route marches and still possess.

This first exercise left me with pleasant memories - of the superb long-distance views over the sea and the hills into China, of the exquisite butterflies - mostly swallowtails, of the smell of the earth in the early morning, of the exotic

Birds Hill. My Platoon Headquarters, with Chang whittling a stick.

and slightly fearsome snakes everywhere, of the hot, sweet, sticky, delicious tea, of the keen and biddable young men with bags of common sense with whom I worked; and of the feel of a tanned and comfortably sore back. The Battalion as a whole learnt many lessons from this first "Scheme" and was able constantly to improve the speed and efficiency with which we manned our defensive positions.

Not long afterwards, my Company decided to attack its own defensive positions on Birds Hill to test their strength. We frequently took out small patrols of a section or platoon to reconnoitre and explore routes to and around our positions in the hills. We found them even more inaccessible from below than we had imagined. It was so jungly and steep that the Company was divided up into small parties to hack their way upwards with machetes. In the cold wet wintry weather, they were often in the clouds, when visibility was at times down to a few feet and one plodded through mud and fought one's way through thick jungle. In general we were satisfied that though not invulnerable, we were sited in as strong a position as was possible.

Life at San Wai

When not in the hills, the soldiers' day started with ten minutes energetic physical training. This was followed by a compulsory Paludrine Parade at which the little pills were handed out, one to each man, as a prophylactic against malaria. As far as I know, despite the prevalence of mosquitoes in the Rains, none of us ever caught malaria in Hong Kong.

After breakfast, other parades followed through the morning to check the cleanliness of the Nissen huts in which the men slept and of their personal kit, and especially of their rifle and other weapons. The men were frequently called out on "fatigues", which might mean unpacking and assembling equipment, cleaning offices and cook-houses, or preparing the parade ground, the church or the officers' or sergeants' messes for some show or other. There were always a thousand odd jobs required to keep the Camp in good order.

When not on fatigues, the men were obliged to do a good deal of 'square-bashing' that is rifle drill on the parade ground below the Camp. They were constantly rehearsing for formal parades that occurred periodically throughout the cooler months. Moreover RSM Webber put the whole Battalion through drill every Friday to ensure we worked together and keep us up to the high standard demanded by the CO. In addition, each company in turn provided the Night and Day Guards at the camp gates and Guards of Honour for visiting dignitaries; and for such performances, we had to insist on plenty of 'bull', requiring the clothing, kit and rifles on display to be impeccable.

More importantly we sought to keep ourselves and everyone fit with a great deal of 'bashing', by which was meant running or jogging along the tracks round the Camp; perhaps a couple of times a week I had to take out my platoon on a run across the paddy or down the Jhelum Valley. When not "bashing", our Platoons spent many hours learning and practising both defensive and offensive fighting; to improve our defences, we dug trenches, built strong points, put out barbed wire, acted as sentries, rehearsed the dawn 'stand-to' and so on; in the offensive role, we spent a great deal of time learning how to throw hand grenades, to use bayonets, to make frontal or flanking attacks, to use and fire the Bren gun and PIAT, and so on. The number of things to learn was endless and the need for constant rehearsal was endless too until men and officers reacted to commands instantly and automatically.

The early afternoons tended to be a bit more sedentary, when the troops were required to listen to lectures on aspects of their work - and personal hygiene - and to conduct TEWTs, a horrible acronym that stood for *"Tactical Exercises without Troops"*, that is to say classroom practice of what could later be performed on the ground. Much of the instruction and direct supervision was done by the NCOs. Each platoon had two or three, overseen by the Company Sergeant Major on whom discipline and efficiency much depended. We young officers were actively involved at every stage in planning and managing the programme, conducting the inspections and delivering the lectures as well as providing suitable leadership, encouragement and discipline as required. We had significant authority over the men and the opportunity to guide and help them in their individual behaviour and personal problems. We had a good deal of paperwork to do reporting regularly with Muster Rolls, on attendance, efficiency and the adequacy of their kit. We had also to carry out regular sick parades - sending those in need of treatment down to Peter Boultbee, the MO.

We had also to do fortnightly pay parades, to ensure all the troops received their due wages in cash - which all too often disappeared swiftly over the weekend in the NAAFI or the bars of Fan Ling and Kowloon. Once a fortnight on a Friday, the paying officer and pay clerk sat behind a table and an NCO called up each soldier in turn. He marched up to the table, saluted, held out his left hand, received his money, signed its receipt in the Imprest Account, took a pace back, saluted, turned and marched off. One weekend I had to do the paying out without the assistance of the pay clerk who was on forty-eight hours leave, and I was $110 up on the Imprest when I came to reconcile the figures. I spent most of the Saturday checking them and much of the Sunday worrying about them. It was with huge relief I tackled the clerk on his return on the Monday and found that the discrepancy was not my fault but his, and the money was not lost but safely elsewhere.

Orderly Officer

All the subalterns took it in turns to be Orderly Officer of the Battalion, and the duty came round every third week. We had to get up in Service Dress and Sam Browne at 6.30am. The first job was to dismount the Guard that had been on duty at the entrance gates all night, and to mount their replacements, the

Battalion Day Guard. We had to do a tour of the barracks, attend the troops' meals in the cook house - and their breakfast was a fairly sordid affair - check various offices during the day, keep an eye on the Guard Room, inspect the Guard during the day and organise the Night Guard in the evening.

At night the Orderly Officer slept in the Adjutant's Office close to the telephone with the outside world, and stayed up to keep the sentries alert and sort out minor problems around the Camp. As an example, I was on duty one weekend evening in December when I had to send the military police out to pick up a Dorset soldier who was making a nuisance of himself in Fan Ling. Then I had to wait up until 2am when a late train, held up after an accident on the line, arrived at the station full of soldiers that had enjoyed a convivial evening in Kowloon.

It was maddening to be Orderly Officer at weekends or on public holidays when one had to stay in Camp in uniform while it emptied itself into Kowloon, and all too many young soldiers came back drunk in the evenings. When working hours changed in the hot weather, the job of Orderly Officer became even less attractive. One had to rise at 6am, dressed in 'JG' to dismount the Guard and mount its successor; one was also obliged to inspect the Night Guard around 1.30am in what was a long day and a short night.

Internal Security

One of the most important duties given to battalions stationed in Hong Kong was to assist in the maintenance of law and order in support of the civil power - the local Police Force. When on 'IS Duty' we went about our normal job, but were on call to back up the Police to quell a riot, break up a disturbance, prevent sabotage or defend vulnerable points, such as power and railway stations, in the event of a bandit attack. For this purpose each battalion in the Brigade took it in turns to stand by for call-out one week in three. One company had to be ready to respond to a request for assistance from the Police at one hour's notice with necessary stores, transport, ammunition, wirelesses and so on; while another company had to be ready with heavier weapons at two hours notice. Those of us involved had to stay in camp - married officers had to come in for the purpose - and have all our kit ready for a pretty swift move.

The police gave us several demonstrations of the conduct of their 'riot squads' when confronted by an angry mob. They had the use of their truncheons, tear gas, the 'sick-making gas' which so amused us in the South China Sea, and 'police guns' which were a type of shot-gun that we were told was painful but harmless when fired. Then when all their resources were spent, if the crowd had not dispersed, they called out the military - and we were equipped with rifles, and after due process might be required to fire them. We officers were impressed with the smartness, discipline and efficiency of the Chinese and Pakistani policemen whom we saw on these demonstrations.

There were occasional call-outs. Not long before our arrival, one company of the Wiltshires had been summoned to go into the hills on a very exciting bandit hunt. When A Company's was on its first 'IS duty', one platoon had to put on its kit and embark in transport when the police in Fan Ling found a store of illicit arms and were uncertain whether they could manage the resulting unrest.

The Korean Reinforcements

The men of the Royal Fusiliers who had come out on the boat with us were destined to join their Regiment in Korea after spending a short period of preparation in our Battalion. They were split up into six platoons in A Company for six weeks' further training. During November and December, I was transferred to A Company to help in this task - I imagine my experience as a trainer at the Depot was thought relevant.

I found myself in charge of a bunch of young cockneys who were quick, tough, lazy and independent-minded as Londoners always used to be - most unlike the Dorset boys in the other companies. My new Company Commander was Bill Heald who had come out with the advance party and I had not met before arriving at the camp. Bill was a huge, affable, highly intelligent and pleasant chap with whom I found it easy to work. He was brave and had won both a DSO and MC during the war. He was also generous, and keen that we all got to know each other; and there was also a quiet and thoughtful side to him that was unlike some army officers I met - Bill told me he had spent time at Batcombe Friary near Sherborne before the war, which I had also visited from school and was able to talk about with him.

Bill's Second in Command was John Sims and together they worked hard to get the Company to bond and work together. Bill generously threw a cheerful evening party for all his officers and NCOs at his home near Fan Ling soon after we started work together. A little while later, he arranged a weekend picnic on Taipo Beach for everyone in the company and their wives and children. Though it was a poor beach beside the railway line, we ate and drank and swam a lot together and strolled through the excessively dirty and smelly fish market. Later still, I took my platoon out in the battalion bus for 3$ each for a swim from the beautiful beach at Repulse Bay at the back of Hong Kong Island; and I've no doubt the other platoon commanders made similar efforts to strengthen the team spirit of their men.

The men in our charge had to be equipped and trained swiftly and effectively before they rejoined their Regiment. Sergeant Creech had been made up to Colour Sergeant and he gave them the highest standard of equipment available to the battalion; and we reckoned the best training for the men would be to take them as often as possible into the hills to learn the hard way to be self-sufficient in their own small units. We had in addition to perform normal company duties within the battalion during 'Brigade Manning' exercises; that is to say, when the other companies went up the hill we had to go too. So we were seldom to be found in the Camp - and this was absolutely right for the sort of war our Fusiliers were preparing to fight.

A Company's defensive position was on a different hill to the one I had previously defended; my platoon of Fusiliers was stuck right out on a narrow rocky ridge which was very difficult to dig into; so we heaped earth on top of our trenches and almost buried the three concrete pill-boxes we inherited up there; and we set about surrounding ourselves with thirty feet of barbed wire - which was a long and nasty job. We went up there twenty-four hours after my attachment and twice within two weeks.

On the second occasion, on Exercise *Heron*, we set off at dawn and reached our position by 9.30am, at the same time as the rest of the Brigade around us, each battalion on its chosen hill, and the Welch battalion on our left flank on the hill called Ti Tan Yang. The Brigadier seemed pleased when he came round to see how we were getting on. As usual we fed ourselves and the mules brought up our food, water, cookers and paraffin, as well as our blankets and nets. The following week we were on our ridge once more and dug out and roofed my platoon HQ with a deep communication trench to the company stores; and we

San Wai mule lines. Loading up for an exercise in the hills.

were able to give an exhibition of digging to the GOC. When we came down from the hills, we also gave him a demonstration of grenade-throwing in a pit at the back of the Camp, and fired our rifles for him on the hundred yards range tucked away there too.

Sha Tau Kok

One of A Company's special responsibilities was the Observation Post at Sha Tau Kok on the last hill before the frontier. Our OP overlooked not only the little border check point on the road into China but also many miles of paddy fields and hills beyond, and one big mountain named Ny Tung San, which with striking originality we called '*China Mountain*'. Whenever we looked at it from the OP, we used to think, "Down there just below us, is 'the enemy'." We were required to have observers on duty 24 hours a day, 7 days a week, and to keep a full hour-by-hour record of what the Chinese were doing on their side of the frontier. The climb up to the OP took over an hour from the milestone dropping-off point on the border road and was steep and rough and hard-going, especially when one was loaded with supplies for the observers and humping a bedding roll on one's shoulders. There was a constant demand for biscuits to give to the coolies who generally popped up whenever one set off up the hillside and offered to carry our loads in exchange for NAAFI rations.

I enjoyed visiting the OP and sometimes slept there with our team of watchers to see what was going on across the frontier. We were often in the clouds, but through binoculars on a clear day we could observe the goings-on in three villages and a small army encampment. On occasions a fully trained unit of fifty men did physical training and field-craft not a mile below our position. We were told that this unit came from North China and was similar to those that were fighting the United Nations forces in Korea.

When the Brigadier said he wanted to see the place, Sgt Ayling, Cpl Foulger and I went up to make sure everything was tidy for him; we spent two full days and nights up there and saw a great deal of the Chinese activities below us; the brass hats never arrived but we had a grand time on the hilltop looking into China.

In December storms, the corrugated iron roof was blown off the top of the OP and the telephone cable torn to pieces; and I was sent up to investigate. I found the gale had given the observers a sleepless night, and I stayed a couple more days to arrange for the roof to be replaced, the cables to be relaid, and the little cookhouse to be repaired where its sides had been crushed, and I came down the hill only when all had been set to rights again. The Chinese over the border were very busy at that time, exercising in steel helmets as if they considered we might be planning to attack them. We left them to it.

The Adjutant gave me orders to go up to the OP early on New Year's Day. So after a couple of hours' sleep following our heavy New Year's Eve Party, I set off at 5.30am in the dark up the hillside. To my horror, on arrival an hour later, I found everybody asleep and the place in a filthy state. I had no alternative but to give severe rockets to the Fusilier corporal who was supposed to be in charge as well as to the man who was supposed to be on watch. I put them both on "a charge" for CO's Orders, and set them the task of cleaning the place up. Later that morning I handed over to my relief and was back in Camp in time for the curry lunch in the Mess. A fortnight later, the CO gave the two defaulters fourteen days CB.

On several later occasions I went up to Sha Tau Kok for the thrill of it. I spent three days up there in early February and gave up a holiday weekend later in the month to improve the trenches and cooking arrangements. I particularly enjoyed sitting at the kitchen fire and talking far into the night with the soldiers taking their turn on watch.

Field Firing

In December A Company spent two long days 'Field Firing' - that is firing with live ammunition in realistic attacks in training for 'the real thing'. We took over the Lo Wu ranges and gave our young Royal Fusiliers as close an experience as we could of infantry fighting in the sort of surroundings they might expect in Korea - in wild rough country that was at that time of year very dry and dusty - rather as it had been on the Lulworth ranges, where I had trained new recruits at the Dorchester Depot earlier in the year.

Soon after that exercise, the Royal Fusiliers in Korea called urgently for reinforcements and we despatched eighty men and two key NCOs to join their Battalion at the front.

Exercise 'Partridge'

It was a Government edict that only those aged over nineteen years could go to Korea, so the younger men stayed behind and were soon joined by another draft that had come out by troopship from England. So it was a fresh group of young men whom we took up the hill on the next exercise. It was even bigger than before and involved the whole Division in the New Territories. Even the RAF joined in. They came over in Vampires and flew disgracefully low over our heads, pretending to dive-bomb us. By then the weather was much colder and we needed all the blankets C/Sgt Creech could lay his hands on, and we still had to sleep in all our clothes on those wind-swept mountain tops. I had a bad time. Having taken out a patrol after dark, I slipped a long way down a bare rock and landed in a heap of barbed wire. However, a much more serious accident occurred when one of our anti-tank gun carriers hit a train at a level crossing at the bottom of Birds Hill jeep track. The MO rushed out and came back later with the sad news that seven young men of the Anti-Tank Platoon had been badly injured and been taken by ambulance to the hospital. That particular Exercise left a bad taste in one's mouth. The Officers' mess was silent that night and we went to bed early shaken by the tragedy.

Only a few days later, I went down to Kowloon to greet yet another new draft of Fusiliers from the Empire Orwell that had just docked. The poor young men looked very green, and were bewildered - as no doubt had we Dorsets when we had arrived three months earlier. I gave them such encouragement as I could and brought them back to Camp to settle in. I then learned to my surprise that the Fusiliers were to have a new set of officers - the old team was moved on. We decided the change had been made because Bill Heald had been too insistent that the Fusiliers should have priority over Dorsets in training and equipment. When the battalion received an issue of 'jungle hats', we demanded to have them in A Company first; when the field-firing range was made available to the Battalion, A Company wanted it in preference to everyone else. So we were all sent packing and Ivor Ramsay was put in charge of the company of reinforcements with a fresh team.

This arrangement did not last long, however. After only a few weeks, the Brigadier ordered A Company to revert to its normal role, and the Royal Fusiliers to be scattered throughout the Battalion in penny packets. This caused a major, and probably unnecessary, upheaval, and lots of problems because they worked to a different training programme to the rest of us, but they settled down again in the end.

Return to D Company

I went back to D Company under John Drew and resumed charge of No 11 Platoon. I went straight up Bird's Hill where the men were spending each day encircling their position with a 15 foot belt of barbed wire. I spent three nights up there with them and brought them down at the weekend for a well-earned break.

In the following weeks we were constantly up in the hills - apart only from a short period around Christmas and the New Year. On a typical day I took the platoon up Ti Tan Yang from the east doing map reading, and split the men up into sections; Cpl Pattenden and his men went one way, Sgt Leach's lot another, Cpl Ballard's people another, and so on. Dick Rowbotham coordinated our climb with his signallers. It was a scramble up over steep rock and through secondary jungle, but we had superb views over China from the top of the mountain where we eventually assembled; and we all came down together in the evening.

Another day, we went on what was called a *"Battalion Skeleton Exercise"*.

The Company marched down the Jhelum Valley and over the low hill called The Bastion. It poured with rain all morning and we were warned of 'enemy' ahead. I and my platoon headquarters were careless and allowed ourselves to be ambushed and wiped out. The CO was waiting for us and brought us back to life on condition we answered correctly some questions on regimental history he had given us when we set off. Fortunately we had sent runners back to base to find the answers and were thus rehabilitated for what turned out to be a long and very wet march back to Camp through Taipo and Fan Ling.

A Night Exercise

Soon after New Year, I spent several hours over three or four days walking the ground for the Company's first night exercise. It was time well spent. We had a long march to reach the hills and waded all day through paddy fields, knee deep in filthy water for the most part. The evening we passed doing what was known as '*mess-tin cooking*'. Each man was given a couple of potatoes, half a dozen sausages and an egg and told to cook them over his own fire. The Dorset boys were not good cooks but nevertheless seemed to enjoy the experience. After nightfall, small groups of men were given compass bearings and maps of different routes and told to find their way home in the dark. I took one party myself and went slap across country. Some of our route was through thick fir plantations where the undergrowth was knee-high - that was not too bad; other areas were bare with sharp and slippery rocks which were difficult and dangerous in the dark; but the worst travelling was through shoulder-high jungle which consisted of thorn bushes, tall spiky cactus plants and palms with ferns and creepers in the gaps. We had to cut our way through with machetes. I slipped head first down a rock-face and was concussed for three days, so was later able to recall little of the last leg of my group's journey home. Our first experience of night work was no fun.

The Penetration Patrol

One of the Battalion's jobs in the New Territories was to fly the flag; that is to make the British army's presence felt in a friendly way among the local Chinese population. To this end, we sent out foot patrols from time to time to go round the villages, talk to the local people, and exchange information and views about local problems.

Immediately after the night exercise, I was delegated to lead one such patrol of ten soldiers round a group of villages in an isolated and wild district on the peninsula on the west coast of the colony. I took two corporals, Pollock and Adams, four privates, Judd, Suter, George and Hodgkins, two signallers and a medical orderly. I was carefully briefed at Brigade HQ, and early one morning we set off by truck for Taipo to collect a police interpreter and a guide. From Taipo jetty we were taken by police launch on an hour's trip across Tolo Bay and through the local fishing fleet of junks to our destination beyond the impenetrable Patsin range. The launch dropped us on a remote beach and we set off on foot. We tramped inland over the hills and across the paddy fields from village to village talking on the way to the headmen and as many people as we could find. We brought medical aid, and showed ourselves as friendly and helpful as possible. In exchange, we asked about the state of crops, cattle, chickens and ducks, health and other troubles, and we gently enquired about the presence of Communists among the local people.

My curiosity took me into many dark huts to shake hands and grin at many elderly and toothless Chinese patriarchs. Their bare-foot, black-robed women largely ignored us and carried on working in their kitchens, while their dirty, ill-behaved children giggled and sniffed. Each village was constructed in brick in a block of half a dozen rooms with lofts on top and walled areas in front where animals and fowl were kept. About sixty people lived in each block, all probably of one family - or at least of one name. They suffered severely from the cold, particularly on the chilly winter nights during our visit. They seemed to have no wool and few means of protection from bitter weather. They looked after their own little valley with its terraced paddy and well-watered vegetable gardens. They grew spinach, sweet potatoes, broccoli, and some sort of asparagus, with a few tangerines, bananas and sugar-cane. There they stayed, never seeing the main road or straying far from their homes.

Their main concern was to protect their crops on which their livelihood depended; they had serious problems with wild pig. We gathered these animals had once been tame but had escaped and gathered in aggressive herds that lived in the jungle on the hill-sides and raided the crops at night. The villagers suffered too from diseases that afflicted their cattle and themselves which they were completely unable to understand. They could not comprehend why we were not always keen to drink the tea they offered us, which, though hot, was without milk, sour and from the Lord knows what source; nor could they grasp our reasons for taking our water from streams before they reached the village, and for using sterilising tablets in our water-bottles. They did not seem to understand our purpose in taking Paludrine. They swallowed a pill greedily enough when we offered it to those said to be suffering from malaria, but I felt they thought it had magical rather than medicinal properties.

I was shown over their temples. They were small shrines where some spirits were reputed to live, and where they regularly burned candles and set off fire crackers to frighten away the worst devils. They also showed me their schools which were clean and airy with maps of the world in Chinese on the walls.

We found no hint of Communism, although I had been warned it was prevalent. They were obviously not completely ignorant or innocent, but I judged they were content with their lot. They lived hard, and, for part of the year worked hard in their rice-fields; they died young but they seemed to be pretty happy, knowing enough about the land they lived on to get a reasonable living out of it, and knowing little about the outside world. At all times, they were friendly and hospitable and gave every appearance of being pleased to see us.

We picked tangerines off the trees round the villages, and paused at a spot called Chung Pi where a beautiful high waterfall ran into a pretty basin that we were told was known as the *"Bridegroom's Pool"*. We stripped off, plunged in and splashed about among large numbers of crabs and lizards. Later we cooked and ate our hot tinned stew, and warmed ourselves beside a huge log fire before turning in for the night. We settled down in a young fir plantation on a hillside above the paddy at Wa Shan Keuk, set up our wireless and found we were in good communication with the Battalion. It was a pleasant evening as we sat on logs round our camp fire chatting of this and that.

I ordered we should all take turns at keeping guard. It was not easy to sleep with noisy crickets and frogs around us, and the hard ground under our ground sheets, but it was not too bad. The next day was steady walking, however, and we were all tired when we emerged eventually on to the main road at Sha Tau Kok Police Station right on the frontier. There we were collected by a 3 ton truck and reached Camp in the late afternoon.

I had an interesting session in the evening being debriefed by Charles Wallis, our Intelligence Officer, and I went to sleep that night dreaming of those strange, scruffy villages and their incredible names. We had landed at Wang Ling, and went to places like Nai Tong Kok, Wu Kau Tang and Ha Tsat Muk Tui.

Exercise Gibraltar 1

It was the army's normal practice in Hong Kong to plan training in a cascading programme of ever bigger and more ambitious exercises through the colder months from October when we arrived until May when the climax would be a Divisional Exercise involving all the troops in the colony. Exercises became more elaborate and ran over three, four and finally five days. By February we were running battalion-level exercises, and the Company took part in a three-day battle, improving our trenches and defending them from the 'enemy' (in the form of the Band and Drums) who gave us no sleep with frequent night attacks. At 5.30am one morning my platoon was over-run by a horde of imaginary Chinamen. I was killed at dawn and our position occupied by the enemy. I jabbered into the wireless to give the impression that the invaders had taken over and heard someone at the other end reading out an impressive casualty list with my name at the head. However I came to life again before breakfast and returned to camp tired, wet and dirty but satisfied with our performance.

Exercise Insomnia

The Company went out on another night exercise that turned out to be a very unhappy experience. I set off down the Jhelum Valley about six o'clock one evening with an advance party and a small group of men who were to act as the 'enemy' for the occasion. I put them in position on a little rocky mound under Cloudy Hill, and at the same time sent the advance party off to recce a route for the attack - but when I returned to the agreed rendezvous they had disappeared without doing their job. The rest of the Company under John Drew marched out down the coast road and, despite the absence of the advance party, put in a very effective night attack according to plan.

It was only after we had reached our objective and I had set off a couple of pounds of gun cotton to signify its destruction, that I realised the men were lost. Retracing our route and searching its length, we came upon the party clustered round one of their number who appeared to have broken his arm following a fall down a rock-face of around thirty feet in the dark. The main body of the Company had six hours march ahead of them, so John took them off in the direction of the Camp, while I went off in the other direction to Taipo to find a vehicle to take our casualty to hospital. I then ran in the pitch dark as fast as I could down a narrow muddy track through several little villages where I searched for help and some form of transport - or at least a bicycle. I banged noisily on the stable door of each Chinese shack that I passed; all the dogs barked; lights went on; I created bedlam, but nobody emerged to offer assistance. I ran on - and on - stumbling over stones and ruts and light-headed with the exertion and the worry. At Taipo, I woke up the village street without success, and struggled up a steep incline to reach the Police Station. To gain entry I had to use their telephone box, and had fearful difficulty making myself understood by the Chinese policeman on the switchboard. At last, after an agony of waiting, a policeman appeared and backed out a land-rover.

We tore back down the track to collect the injured man. His mates had put him on a piece of corrugated iron, strapped him down with tape normally used to mark the route, and lifted him down the hillside to the road. So we were able to shove him in the back of the land-rover and drive him down to the nearest military dressing station. Leaving him in a drugged sleep, I returned to pick up the stretcher-bearers and march them home, reaching camp at about 4.30am. I then turned round and walked back to meet the main body of the Company which was still some way away marching steadily back to base. I was menaced by a pack of pi-dogs that were roaming the paddy, so I waited for the Company by the roadside while dawn broke. When they finally turned up, I rejoined them. We marched in to Camp behind the Band in good order, and we sat down thankfully for breakfast - one of the biggest I ever had.

Acting Company Commander

Though very junior, I had to act as Commander of D Company for three periods in the early months of 1953. In the New Year, John Drew damaged his leg in a rugger match against the Gunners, so Dick Rowbotham and I had to lead the Company during *Exercise Bracken*. With no time to take stock, we were plunged into an exercise testing the Battalion's speed and efficiency of movement if the Chinese crossed the frontier. At four o'clock in the morning we dug the Company out of bed and had them in position in the local village by five. It was dark and cold; the paddy fields were full of wet ditches that we could not see, and our wireless sets did not work; however the Brigadier turned out and was complimentary, so all was well.

A few days later, I was in sole command when the Governor of Hong Kong, Sir Alexander Grantham, paid us a visit, and I was required to find the Guard of Honour from within D Company. HE said he was pleased with all he saw, as indeed he ought to have been for we worked hard to put on a good show for him.

On a later occasion at a time when it was starting to grow very hot and wet in the hills, I was again on my own in charge for Exercise *"Quick March"*. Dick Rowbotham was off on detachment; I was short of NCOs for various reasons, and John Drew was on leave following the birth of his daughter. I took the Company up to Birds Hill and held our positions in good order for the day and night that was required of us.

I went out to John's home in Sek Kong to receive his briefing, congratulate Maisie and admire their new daughter. I rejoiced in such a pleasant change from Mess food and conversation. Not long afterwards, I was invited with others of John's colleagues to the new church at Sek Kong to attend the little girl's christening, which was a very happy occasion.

The snag on these occasions was that the paperwork piled up in the Company Commander's in-tray. Over Easter I had no holiday because of a backlog of typing that had to be sorted out before John returned from leave. I found myself obliged to do complicated jobs like re-writing Standing Orders, overseeing Parade States and mastering the mass of reporting and accounting that the army has always relished. This was quite new to me, and I spent much time and unlooked-for effort in trying to keep track of the bumf as well as commanding the men in the Company.

Exercise Merlin

This was a Brigade scheme involving all three Battalions. Tim Ealand relieved me of command and took over D Company temporarily in John Drew's absence. Tim and Anne had come out by sea to rejoin the Battalion, shortly before this Exercise and I knew them well from our days together in the Dorchester Depot. We had had many friendly conversations together since his arrival and shared a long scramble up Birds Hill one Saturday afternoon soon afterwards at San Wai when we inspected new mortar positions dug by the Assault Pioneer Platoon for which he was then responsible. I was able to work easily with Tim, but on *Merlin* we were set a daunting task.

The whole Battalion set off on a Sunday night to march into the hills north of Taipo. We slept under the stars, but were comfortable and well fed while waiting for supplies to come up by lorry. We were in fine fettle when we moved off at 3am on Tuesday morning to take from the 'enemy' the high ridge that ran southward for fifteen or so miles only twenty yards wide at times in a series of bumps and hillocks, down to the reservoirs above Kowloon. Grassy Hill (2100 feet) and Needle Hill (1,800 feet) were the main objectives in our route forward. One company went forward in turn to attack and capture each feature on the ridge and to pass the rest of the battalion through. Of eight assaults made on the first day which lasted from dawn until 5 o'clock in the evening, D Company led on six occasions. We had no lunch that day and carried heavy packs on our backs - and I had a pickaxe as well and had my work cut out to lead the way.

We found it relatively easy to take Grassy Hill which was Dartmoor country, where I led the Company through the scrub and rocks, flinging thunder-flashes and curses at the retreating 'enemy' (part of the Royal Norfolk Regiment).

We then camped in a wild landscape, well beyond the reach of jeeps, but a few mules were able to straggle up with our necessaries. In our packs we had our washing things, a pullover, a blanket, groundsheet, mosquito net and a few tins of food. Water bottles, empty by the time we had finished, hung from our belts. We relied on the mules for the remainder of our supplies; that is "Compo" rations, water, cookers and petrol, and another blanket if we were lucky - my platoon was never lucky. We were also supported by some gallant coolie porters who brought up the inflammable petrol which mules were not allowed to carry. We were adequately fed, but found it cold at night, and there was so much 'Standing-to' and 'Sentry-go' that we had little chance to sleep or even notice the cold.

The second day of the exercise was much the same as the first, except that we were even shorter of water and I was more on my own. My Platoon assaulted Needle Hill which rose some 500 feet straight up - a real needle - and which was impassable even to the mules, (or *'unmuleable'* as the Regimental Journal had it),

Exercise Merlin. Grassy Hill.

and I had to consolidate my men beyond it and settle for the night in a completely inaccessible spot. So we drew our water from a stream, sterilised it, 'brewed up' on a wood fire, and slept soundly from exhaustion under a single blanket.

Like all the men that slept those nights on the hills and ran and 'fought' over and up them, I think I enjoyed it. I enjoyed learning about the chaps, their humour, capabilities and attitudes to life; I did not mind roughing it; I was pleased with each successful action and well-planned attack; I thoroughly relished leading and guiding forty odd men for several days very much on our own. I learnt on that exercise what it was like to be really tired, really dirty, and really thirsty - not just feeling like a glass of beer, but actually needing water to keep going. More important, I learnt how to lead men. I had a platoon of keen soldiers under my command in the field, as near to being in action as one would ever get; for how they fed, fought, marched and slept depended on me.

We left the hills before dawn on Thursday morning and came down to the air strip at Sha Tin on the Kowloon road where we returned to civilisation. There, instead of cooking for ourselves, we were supplied with a 'slap-up' meal

Exercise Merlin, Needle Hill.

by the Field Cooks, and with hot shaving water - a wonderful luxury. Then we embarked on landing-craft which took us round the coast to Taipo on a pleasant sea trip, although the police boats leaked and left us wading ankle-deep on the duck boards. We were in high spirits, however, and marched back from Taipo as a Battalion singing and whistling led by the CO, with the Band playing at the head of the column. Surprised villagers looked out of their cottages and up from their ploughing to see a body of 700 unwashed weary men slogging homewards. The only thing that dampened our ardour on return was to see the flags at half-mast and to hear of the death of Queen Mary. As was the custom, we went into mourning, cancelled social engagements, and put on black ties and black armbands for several days.

Exercise Osprey

The last exercise of the spring, marking the end of the training season, took place in early April, when happily John Drew was back from leave. Over 24 hours the Dorsets from the CO down to the humblest rifleman were tested by the Brigadier and his staff as to whether we were fit to go to war or not. We were caught out, however, for the rains started early, and did not stop for some days. We had neither food nor sleep and were wet throughout the day and night of the Scheme. We left Camp at 2 o'clock on a Wednesday afternoon and were given a series of hills to take and prepare to defend against counter-attack before dark. We failed badly; my men were still stumbling about looking for their kit on the hillside an hour after dark; no food came up to us, and no mosquito nets arrived. The rations that we were supposed to take up the hills on our backs were 24-hour packs of half a dozen tins with little Napthaline cookers. But that evening we went hungry. Worse still, as soon as I had settled the men down, I was told to take a ten-man section out a couple of miles as an outpost "Standing Patrol" for the night. We lay up in a haystack in the middle of a Chinese village and watched all the paths back to our positions. Understandably, noisy chow dogs resented our presence, and barked at us all night long, so it was a futile exercise.

No sooner had my patrol got back at dawn next morning than I found the whole Battalion was moving on. We commandeered every truck we could find and were lifted across the Colony to Un Long where we were given the job of driving a number of 'bandits' into the sea by 5pm - again a race against time. The country over that side was flatter and we moved very fast, did a successful pincer movement and trapped our 'bandits' (a company of one of the other Battalions), made them prisoners, and were in the trucks on the way home before tea.

The Hot Weather

The temperature warmed up fast that April, and the Brigadier's idea was to require us all to rise early to do as much as we could before the sun rose, and to finish at 2 o'clock in the afternoon in order to escape the hottest hours. Reveille was at 0545hrs, and we did three periods of training before breakfast at 0900hrs. We started again at 1000hrs and were supposed to pack the rest of the day's training in before 1345hrs. (Sensibly, the routine was changed in June to give the men breakfast at 0700hrs, and a short NAAFI break mid morning.) Either way, sport was much curtailed and was tolerable only in the first and last hours of daylight. Unless we were on parade, we lived and worked in shorts and boots without shirts particularly when in the barrack rooms and camp offices where the fans were inadequate in the extreme heat.

The problem was that all the married men shot off back to Kowloon at 1400hrs for their late lunch, and those of us staying in the Camp lost the chance to sort things out with them. Moreover, if one did not complete one's office work by lunch-time, one missed the meal - and that was frequently my situation.

It was necessary to keep out of the sun in the early afternoon - there were all sorts of stories about the dire effects of the Hong Kong climate on those who overdid it. When I visited the BMH in mid-June, I found thirty Dorsets there with one trouble or another. I was told of two young Ulster riflemen who had collapsed with heat stroke in the hills in a wiring party with a gang of coolies. One had, sadly, been DOA at hospital; the other's temperature had risen to 110 degrees; and they had put ice on him, put him in an iron lung and given him artificial respiration for several hours without success. Hong Kong was not a nice place to be out of doors for long stretches at the height of summer. I was lucky myself; I had one half day off with heat-stroke early on, and no more than two days off with heavy colds, but there was quite a lot of pneumonia and fearsome tummy troubles from time to time among my fellow officers.

On notice for Korea

On 10th April, a telegram reached the CO from the War Office saying, "*1 DORSET will go to Korea in mid-1954.*" As we paraded the men and told them, we were greeted with a cheer. It was amazing what a difference it made to morale, even when only half those present would be able to go, and we all knew the war was drawing to a weary close. It was then - and doubtless still is - the ambition of every Battalion to enter a theatre of war in order to do the job for which it existed and had been trained, while the main aim of nearly every soldier was to prove his worth in battle.

When I heard the news, I was tempted to sign on for another year. I seriously thought of committing myself to accompanying the Battalion to Korea - which I viewed as a once-in-a-lifetime opportunity. I was enjoying a subaltern's life. I was by then the longest serving Second Lieutenant in the Battalion. I was frustrated that my promotion to full Lieutenant did not come through, although several of my contemporaries received 'accelerated promotion' in April. I had also discovered that there were many silly irritations in a junior officer's work, and I learned that some jobs one was required to do could be massively boring. Despite these concerns, I thought it was a good life for a young man. I felt I was successful in my work of training young soldiers; I thought I was able to teach them things that were useful to them, help them to have more worthwhile lives and achieve their potential, as well as becoming useful soldiers. I shared the opinion expressed by several of my senior colleagues that, while nine tenths of the soldier's existence was monotonous, it was worth enduring in order that one could share in that last one tenth which was the most worthwhile thing anyone could do.

I wrote a long letter to my father asking for advice, saying I was thoroughly enjoying my life and work as a soldier, that I should like to stay in the Army, and I thought I would be doing something useful; but on the other hand, I recognised I was committed to Cambridge and had a great opportunity there that I would be stupid to turn down. My parents wrote back hurriedly to dissuade me. By the time I received their letters, however, I had already had second thoughts. Cambridge was drawing me into its net; and besides I remembered the young Fusiliers we had trained and sent to fight on the Korean front. To remind myself of the realities, I wrote in my diary the strange sad poem by Anne Finch, the Countess of Winchilsea. I wonder if she was mourning the loss of someone she loved in Marlborough's wars.

> "Trail all your pikes, dispirit every drum,
> March in slow procession from afar,
> Be silent, ye dejected men of war!
> Be still the hautboys, and the flute be dumb!
> Display no more, in vain, the lofty banner;
> For see! Where on the bier before ye lies
> The pale, the fall'n, the untimely sacrifice
> To your mistaken shrine, to your false idol, Honour."

- and I thought better of the whole idea. So I did not then pursue the plan of staying on. Our work at San Wai took on a wholly different purpose, however. We were training ourselves no longer simply in a defensive role, but as a battalion soon to go to war requiring all the fighting skills.

In charge again

At the beginning of May, John Drew was transferred to a desk job in FARELF, Dick Rowbotham took charge of a group of soldiers doing guard duty in Kowloon, and I found myself on my own, once more in charge of D Company, and much busier than before. I enjoyed the added responsibility of command, but did not like the paperwork, the forms and returns that seemed to swamp the Company office. Moreover, despite the heat and rain and the end of the training season, we still had to keep our Anti-Mao trenches in the hills in good order. They filled rapidly with water and slime and frequently caved in under the heavy rain. Armed with picks and shovels, I took the Company up each morning before breakfast for several days to repair our positions. We were normally caught by the first shower of the day as we were climbing the hill, so were soaked on arriving at our positions which were often in the clouds. We stripped down to shorts, boots and short socks, and did what digging was possible, returning down the hill in the early afternoon. The heavy rain alternated with very hot sun; neither was pleasant; and our progress in improving our trenches was slow. I had seventy men under my command in the hills that week.

I took the weekly pay parades. When the Company provided the Guard at Flagstaff House, the home and offices of the Commander British Forces, General Sir Terence Airey, I brought down their pay and mail and so forth - and was impressed with their smartness and thought they did a good job under the eye of my fellow subaltern, Dick Rowbotham.

Lo Wu

The Brigade's rifle ranges were at Lo Wu alongside the extensive 'Field Firing' area in a long valley surrounded by hills just our side of the border. All the infantry battalions took it in turns to use these ranges. On several occasions early in my tour I was asked to go out there when other battalions were doing firing practice. I was invited as a 'Neutral Officer', to see fair play and invigilate competitive shooting. It was a boring business but the hosts generally provided hospitality in their mess afterwards and we always finished up with a beer or two.

It was late in the season before it was the turn of the Dorsets. Each Company was allotted the ranges for five days and required to put every man through a series of tests, firing his rifle and a Bren gun to a specified standard - otherwise he would lose some pay. To do it properly, all officers, NCOs and men had to fire three times with each weapon at targets at several different ranges, and it was a long business. We started each day around 7.30am, which meant getting up a good hour and half earlier, and we got back at about 6 o'clock each evening. On return, the officers had an hour's accumulated office work, while the soldiers had to clean their guns and have them inspected for cleanliness before they could have their meal; so the day's work was seldom over before 9pm.

We were on the ranges from a Friday solidly over a weekend until the following Tuesday, and it was not far short of a nightmare. Every morning the rain came down, soaking us all and churning up the paths and the firing-points to mud, the tents leaked and the organisation was spoilt by the weather, but we had to press on in order to get everyone through in the time allotted to us.

Fortunately, we completed our programme just on schedule, with scores that were good in comparison with other Companies - my own were just creditable. We even had time at the end to practise a team which we entered in the Battalion Rifle Meeting. Dick Rowbotham was a good shot and led the Company into second place in the Company Shield in appalling weather, while Sgt Leach, and Cpls Hobbs and Chappell did well in the Battalion Individual Championship, thereby bringing credit to the Company that trained them - young Hobbs was our best shot. It was a relief to have that job behind us. Apart from anything else, one weekend and three KD shirts were ruined.

Night-firing

Later in the year we tried out a new idea on the ranges - night firing. We went out after dark, Cpl Pattenden rigged up electric bulbs to batteries on circuits so that they flashed on and off over the target; Cpl Webb and Dick and I stood by with verey pistols and mortar flares and had a grand time setting them off while the soldiers tried to fire at a half visible target. It was a good test of skill and alertness, and I enjoyed it - until I fell into a monsoon ditch and hobbled about for the rest of the night.

Visit of CinC FARELF

I think the only time General Keightley came to inspect us was in the middle of June, and it was a day when I was unwell. I had a smashing headache on waking that morning, but by 0700 hrs was in the Company lines rehearsing weapon training in preparation for the General's visit. At 0900 hrs I escaped briefly and looked in on the MO. I had a temperature of 100.6 and was told to go to bed. At 1045 hrs we resumed work on the Company 'WT Circus'. An hour later the CinC arrived in a flurry of brass hats. We performed as required; he approved our display. He left at 1205 hrs; ten minutes later I took to my bed and slept round the clock.

Exercise Festubert

On the day following the CinC's visit, the battalion had the task of running an elaborate TEWT for a Brigade Officers' Day at which they all came up to the Mess and in small teams we studied the subject of 'Withdrawal'. Festubert is the name of the village in France where the 2nd Dorsets found themselves surrounded during the retreat to Dunkirk while acting as part of the rearguard. After losing many men and their heavy equipment, the remnants of the gallant battalion had to withdraw by night and just slipped through the net closing around them. Knocker chose the title and we had to perform a little play to illustrate the way our predecessors had escaped the noose. Ivor Ramsay had served with the 2nd Battalion in that disastrous campaign and spoke with some authority. My part was very small, and I fear I spent the morning grumbling at having to miss my breakfast. It was deemed a great success however, and it was the final exercise of any sort in which I was involved.

Handing over

The third anniversary of my joining up was 4th September 1953. Assuming a four week return journey by troopship, my departure from the Battalion was presumed for early July. Awaiting news of departure and hand-over, I carried on running the Company as the sole officer, keeping everyone busy and reasonably fit, while also keeping the paper moving in the Company Office.

In late May I received ten day's notice to return home on the Empire Orwell leaving Hong Kong at the beginning of June. I was in a fearful flap about such a rushed programme, and fortunately the CO wanted me to stay on a little longer. He wished me to remain in charge of the Company to provide continuity over the period of the Annual Inspection of the Battalion and to hand the Company over properly to a newly-arrived more senior officer during the second week of June. This was Steve Elvery who had been TA Adjutant at the Depot with me, and whom I had known well from Dorchester days. He had come out by sea to join the Battalion early in April, and was taking time to familiarise himself with the Battalion's role before taking over from me. I was pleased with this arrangement, and was then put on the Empire Clyde sailing on 4th July. A little later, another flap occurred when my name was taken off the Clyde passenger list for unknown reasons. I was told I was reinstated only when on my last exercise in the hills within a few days of sailing.

Steve and I started the hand-over with a tour and inspection of the D Company dispositions on Birds Hill. Over two very wet days, we took the Company up and showed Steve round our communications, trenches, wire and other defences. We took advantage of the visit to test our signal and wireless equipment. For one last time, I had great fun bringing down (imaginary) mortar fire on various (imaginary) enemy locations until we were over-run by them.

The Annual Inspection

Steve and I had to prepare hurriedly for the Annual Inspections to be made - first by the Brigadier of the battalion's paper-work, and secondly by the General of our fighting ability. We spent a weekend going through our Company's books and putting them straight. I regret Steve found a lot wrong when we went through them together, and he told me so - which depressed me as I had done my best as a locum with my limited experience - but we presented a united and shining face to the Brigadier when he came round. He sat in the Company Commander's chair and said, *"I want to see this and this and this."* We were able to produce everything he wanted. He looked at the Parade State in Steve's (formerly my) office, and seemed content. He then went into the Arms Store and found it clean and in order; and he went away seemingly well satisfied with us - though we gathered the Battalion Orderly Room was not so clever at bluffing.

When the GOC came round the Battalion, D Company was required to demonstrate rifle-handling on the ranges. The General was reputed to go round looking for faults, and not be satisfied until he found something wrong. He would turn to a Company Commander and demand:

"*When did your company last fire a mortar bomb?*"

"*Last week, Sir!*"

He would then address the first private soldier he met with the same question, and receive the reply, "*Never zee'd un, zur!*"

Or he would enquire, "*When did you last inspect your soldiers' socks?*"

"*We do it once a fortnight, Sir!*" And the first socks he would ask to see would have enormous holes in them.

Out on the ranges we had everything laid out according to the copy-book, when the General breezed up with a huge following of brass and red tabs. I had some soldiers on one side balancing pennies on their rifles in order to test the steadiness of their grip. This impressed him as he could not imagine where the pennies had come from - in fact they were from a money box I kept for Susan[1]. The General then looked at our records showing all the firing we had done over the preceding three months. This was a respectable document and pleased him. So off he went in the direction of the Mule Lines (the next object on show), purring all over. Sadly, I never saw the pennies again and the money box was rather emptier after the visitation than before.

Exercise Teacup

On my last Sunday afternoon, the CO and Brigadier were summoned to Headquarters and all troops were confined to Camp. Rumours flew around; all plans for the weekend and week ahead were cancelled; and the CO returned to tell us we were to mobilise in preparation for a move to Korea, with a deadline to be ready to move on 12th July. We knew that, despite the peace talks, the Chinese had launched a fierce assault on American and Commonwealth forces in South Korea, while at the same time the South Korean President Rhee had stupidly ordered his guards to release all North Korean prisoners of war who did not want to be repatriated. All hell had been let loose and there was a massive job to be done to round up the North Koreans wandering around the south of

1   Susan is the daughter of my brother John and his wife Doreen, born in November 1951.

the country. At much the same moment, to our great relief, news came through of the release of men of The Glosters (many of them National Servicemen) who had been made prisoners of war after the battle of the Imjin River in horrifying circumstances. Plans were laid urgently for repatriation of the former POWs by sea, while we were all reminded of the dangers and hardship of the fighting in Korea.

I was tempted once more. Without much thought and without consulting those at home, I told the CO I would like to cancel my sea passage on the Clyde and remain with the Battalion - at least until late September. I then tackled John Archer and expressed my earnest wish to stay on. He and the CO had been obliged to reorganise the battalion in preparation for mobilisation. They created a new unit called Y Company, to which were transferred soldiers under the age of 19, those due to leave the Colony soon and other "ineligibles". I found myself in limbo.

I carried on doing my job and handing over my platoon to the new arrival, Peter Pearmain. I was sent down to the BMH to find out how our sick were faring and who among those in bed would be fit enough to rejoin the Battalion by the deadline. I acted for the last time as Orderly Officer on 1st July, mounted the Guard at 8.15am, inspected the men's breakfast, and did all the usual checks and inspections all day.

I saw the CO again to press my case, but I dare say he had weightier things on his mind. All the soldiers were told to pack their kit; company files and furniture were put away; the Officers Mess was packed up; curtains and cushion covers were folded away, and the silver and glass were wrapped in packing cases. Meantime I paid D Company's bills and closed the company accounts ready for a rapid audit. I rang the Adjutant that evening and was told that a message had just come through,

"No National Service officer or man may extend his service for the purpose of Exercise Teacup."
"Is that final?"
"Yes!"

So that was that; I was part of Y Company. I thought what a daft name to give such a key exercise, and began hurriedly to prepare to close my service with the 1st Battalion.

With hindsight it would have been absurd for me to have stayed any longer in Hong Kong. Not only did the Battalion remain in San Wai for a further twelve months, but the returning prisoners of war took priority on the troopships returning home for several months; and I should have risked losing my place at Cambridge if I had missed the July boat, or been obliged to fly back to the UK without baggage and in some discomfort because of transport difficulties.

Birthday bumps

Chapter 4

Hong Kong: Social Life and Leisure

🍊 🍊 🍊

If you've 'eard the East a- callin', you won't never 'ave naught else.

From *Mandalay* by Rudyard Kipling

🍊 🍊 🍊

The Officers' Mess
The Mess was both the group of men with whom I lived and worked, and the collection of buildings where we ate, slept and relaxed. A central block at the highest point of the Camp comprised the ante-room, dining room that ran the full width of the building, bar, billiard room and offices. Below the main building, wooden shacks that were our bedrooms spread out along terraces on a gently sloping hill. A terrace ran round the building where we sat when the evenings were warm, and on special occasions listened to the Regimental Band. Behind the Mess was our one and only bathroom of a flimsy construction. Its thin wooden walls caught fire one January evening from over-heated pipes, and several panels of one wall were destroyed; and for some weeks we had to bathe in full view of passing members of the staff until the miserable building was repaired.

Bachelor officers had quarters in the mess while the more senior men who were married and accompanied by their wives and families used its facilities infrequently for formal occasions and parties. Knocker, the CO, and one or two other older men who were 'unaccompanied' shared our accommodation while conscious of their seniority and likely to boss us youngsters about - though always ready to unbend after dinner when they shared the informal atmosphere of the ante-room and billiard room. The Mess had a good atmosphere and the officers who were my daily companions got on with each other amazingly well, considering how closely we were thrown together.

Each resident officer paid 2/6d a day towards his meals which was added to the standard army rations supplied by the RASC and enabled the Chinese cooks to feed us pretty well. They produced two fried eggs and bacon for every officer for every breakfast - and I never wanted to see a fried egg again when I came home. They also insisted on providing banana sandwiches with a cup of tea when we came in after work at 4 o'clock every afternoon - and I certainly have never looked a banana sandwich in the face again. Their *tour de force* was curry in many shapes, sizes and tastes. For Sunday lunch in the Mess they put in a generous portion of chillies together with a glorious mixture of strong flavours, and we were lucky to have the afternoon in which to cool down.

Resident subalterns were given bedrooms in half a shack, furnished with a big fan in the ceiling, a fireplace, wardrobe, chest of drawers, and desk in addition to the single bed under its mosquito net. In addition to taking Paludrine every morning, we slept under the mosquito nets and kept the gauze anti-bug windows closed after dark. As it grew warmer, we switched on the fans to cool the air all day and night, but at times, unpleasantly fierce winds blew through the Camp and made our rooms thoroughly uncomfortable.

Douglas Jenks and I had adjoining halves of one of the shacks on the top terrace - which was conveniently close to the main Mess building and the bathroom. I used to listen to Douglas' wireless to hear the late news through the thin wooden wall that separated our rooms. We lent each other books from time to time but Douglas' library was far above my head; I borrowed from him *"The Unquiet Grave"* by 'Palinurus' (Cyril Connolly), which I never understood.

My monthly mess bill for liquid refreshment varied between £12/10/= (that was $200) and around £17, which was half the money that I originally arranged to go into my local bank account. At first, I had to try and economise sharply - which was very difficult over the Christmas season - until I managed to open an account with the Hong Kong and Shanghai Bank in Kowloon, and have money transferred into it from Lloyds in Luton. Things only became easier when my Tropical Kit Allowance and Local Overseas Allowance came through.

Each officer had a batman drawn from his platoon to perform the dual roles of platoon wireless operator when on exercises and personal servant when in the Camp. If the batman made my life a little easier in the Mess, he played an essential role on exercises. Not only did he sort out my tent and food, he also organised our radio communications with the outside world, and he thus enabled me to go round the Platoon organising their dispositions, and supervising their work on the trenches. A young man named Wareham looked after me for a while and was good on the wireless; he was followed by a fellow named Long who was an equally proficient operator and my right hand man when I was excessively busy as Acting Company Commander.

It is worth noting that my status while in Hong Kong was always slightly ambiguous. I was in my third year of service, and had completed two years as a Second Lieutenant; I was treated as if I were a Regular Officer without the promotion to First Lieutenant that normally came at that time. For example, I was required, along with the other Regulars, to write an essay one winter weekend - a strange army tradition dating back to the days when one had nothing to do during the long dark evenings. I chose to write on *"The advantages of regular recruitment"*, felt very out of practice at essay-writing, and spent half a Sunday in February staring at a blank sheet of paper. Only when I brought a drink down from the Mess, did I at last start scribbling, and with a glass in hand I finished the essay at 1 o'clock on Monday morning.

Officers' Dress

On our arrival we thought how pleasant was the weather - not unlike a good English summer. We wore our battledress for normal daytime wear. For formal parades and the like, we put on Service Dress; and in the evenings on Mess Nights we dressed in our "Blues". When, in early December the climate changed sharply for the worse, we piled on the sweaters, dug out blankets for our beds, and lit fires in our rooms. A strong cold wind blew through the anti-mosquito gauze netting which did the duty of glass in our windows, and a permanent drizzle and mist clouded our valley. I sent off home for my duffle coat which my mother nobly packed up for me though, regrettably, it took three months to reach me.

In April, as it grew warmer, the General decreed that the Army would go into tropical kit for the summer. We shook the spiders and lizards out of our shirts and shorts; we then dug out all the kit we had worn on the boat and took it down to the tailor to get him to put on the latest embellishments demanded by the CO; the contractor worked his men all night while we offered frantic bribes. We wore khaki shorts, shirts, hose-tops and puttees for work during the day (and slacks after sundown as an anti-malarial precaution). Up in the hills and on exercises we shed our shirts in the heat of the day, but kept on our floppy jungle hats, and our backs soon became brick red from exposure to the sun and wind.

For parades we went into tropical kit, which was an olive green 'bush jacket' worn outside shorts (known as Jungle Green or JG) and we looked quite smart with a Sam Browne on parade.

We carried swords on formal occasions and had periodic sword drill under the RSM which I loathed. In the summer evenings we wore "Red Sea Order", that was 'Blues' trousers, white shirt, bow tie, and cummerbund. For formal evening wear, we added short white jackets known as 'monkey jackets'. For the Governor's Garden Party, we had to buy 'No 3 Dress' which consisted of white trousers and a high-collared starched white jacket.

San Wai Officers' Mess. In tropical kit outside my room. Cap Badge Hill behind me.

Messing Officer

On top of my company duties I had been lumbered by the Adjutant with this job. I found it was a tedious and time-consuming business. My main function was deceptively easy - to issue to the Contractor our rations as provided for the Mess by the RASC. There was much more to it, however. On arrival I had to sort out accommodation, oversee a big clean-up, unpack and stow away numerous boxes of silver and glass, check endless lists, put all the Mess furniture in its place, and plan ahead for feeding my fellow officers and our frequent guests. Soon after our arrival, a new billiard table was delivered by the NAAFI, and it was my job to see it properly installed.

Another of the Messing Officer's jobs was to make up all the mess bills at the end of each month. It was tedious work and kept me up until midnight on the last few days of the month. I tended to spend all my time in those early months with the Fusiliers and neglected my messing duties; I received a sharp rocket from Reggie Hill who in addition to being 2 i/c was also PMC. I had to tear myself away from A Company to arrange belatedly for the decoration of the billiard room with its new table. The room looked good when finished, but meant a lot of work. A few weeks later I was found to have failed to do lots of silly little things, like keeping a check on the Mess furniture and having coat-hooks put up in the cloakroom. I was in bad trouble and was given a reprimand by the CO and another by the PMC for my failings as Messing Officer. So I had to take time off from an exercise and come down from the hills in order to carry out a complete check of all furniture and equipment, including all that had been loaned to the Mess from the quartermaster's stores. Numerous items were found to be missing including enormous pieces like wardrobes and beds which officers had quietly carried off to their offices about the Camp for their personal use.

Perhaps my most important task was to buy Christmas provisions for the Mess. I had to visit the shops and stores in person, because our telephone communications with the Island and Kowloon were feeble and maddeningly erratic. One could be on the phone for an hour trying to contact the NAAFI shop for groceries. Having got through, one would find oneself talking to a Chinese who knew just one word of English, probably "yes", which he would use in every conversation. After spending half an hour talking at him down the phone trying to get into his head that you wanted ten dollars' worth of prawns, you could be sure that the NAAFI van would deliver a dozen tins of marmalade next day.

So off I went to Sek Kong to call at the "engleesh" shops there. I found the turkeys to be frozen and rather droopy; I managed to find sufficient whisky and crackers for everyone, and bought most of the usual festive trimmings, but was completely unable to buy any Christmas decorations. I had to go down to Fan Ling Market and take what little there was on the stalls. Chinese fireworks and crackers were available everywhere - of the sort that bang like squibs to ward off evil spirits - so I bought lots of those to liven up the evenings. It all turned out reasonably well, and as there was plenty to drink, I heard no complaints.

Then, horror of horrors, I had to prepare the mess account books for their annual audit at the year-end. I was required to calculate depreciation on furniture and square all the books. This kept me busy through much of the holiday period. Worse still, in the New Year, we had an outbreak of dysentery among both officers and the British Mess staff. I bought quantities of DDT, blitzed the cockroaches, and worked hard to persuade the Chinese cooks to use soap and water. Relief came only at the end of January when my term of office ended. It was a weight off my shoulders.

In June, perhaps rashly, I offered to take over the job of Mess Wines Officer while Douglas Jenks was on leave. It turned out to be another tedious chore; it meant two hours work on many evenings completing the Daily Wines Sheet and checking that sufficient liquor remained in the bar for the following days. I used to trudge up to the Mess Office, order sandwiches and beer, and settle down to some hard work recording our considerable consumption of alcohol. I was relieved to be able to hand the job back to Douglas on his return from leave.

Dinner Nights in the Mess

The CO decreed frequent Guest Nights to which guests were invited, when we wore Blues in the 'winter' and white monkey jackets in the 'summer'. As Messing Officer, I had to work out each meal with the compradore, and clear the menu with the PMC or other senior officer present. Our guests were often a mix of subalterns and more important officers from other battalions and in staff jobs. They were generally good value; and the conversation was often interesting. 'Shop' was not allowed; and, perhaps sadly, none of the older men ever talked about their experiences in the War, but some of the guests had good stories to tell, and I learned much at the many evening discussions in the Mess.

At one end of the table sat the President for the night, and 'Mr Vice' at the other. The port went round, and toasts were drunk. Meanwhile, the Band played in the ante-room - or outside on warm evenings - and because the Battalion had spent time in Austria, we sang endlessly German marching songs mixed with interminable vulgar ones like *"Me no likee Blitish sailor..."* and others taking us back to the West Country like *"Where be yon blackbird to?"* and the *"The Farmer's Boy"* which was the Regiment's theme song. I fear I sometimes grew rather bored with all the shouting and singing.

The Band also played excellent dance music and had a repertoire of Scottish reels which kept our guests happy. When the Band had gone to bed, it was the long-established custom for my fellow officers to perform silly 'turns' - Gerald Blight was able to keep the party going far into the night, Bill Heald had an entertaining Swazi Warrior sacrificial act - but I am afraid I was hopeless. I enjoyed much more the energetic and sometimes violent games that were the custom late at night. Billiards Fives was played with one's hands instead of cues. It tended to ruin the cushion on the billiard table and was a dangerous game that led to a good many bruises and strains. One of the roughest games was Hicockalorum - fighting piggyback - which generally caused considerable damage to one's clothing if not to the mess furniture. Another local sport was throwing up empty tins of Players cigarettes into the big brass ceiling fans and dodging them as they ricocheted off the spokes and hurtled round the room with amazing violence. When all else failed, we would throw rolls of lavatory paper into the fans in the billiard room - it flew everywhere and made a fearful mess.

Remembrance Day 1952

The presence of so many other battalions gave plenty of opportunities for joint celebrations of one sort and another. On November 11th, we held our Remembrance Day Service jointly with the Royal Ulster Rifles at a Drumhead Service on the parade ground that lay between our two camps. We remembered and honoured the many British servicemen who had lost their lives in the fighting in Korea the previous year. This was perhaps the first occasion on which

San Wai Officers' Mess. In mess kit, playing games after a dinner night.

we met and mingled with the RUR officers who came up to our mess for a drink afterwards. We were their guests on a number of subsequent occasions, as they had a big hall that converted into a cinema where we saw several amusing films.

Ferozeshah Day

In mid-December Dorset officers were invited to a big parade by the Wiltshire regiment to commemorate the battle of Ferozeshah (in the First Sikh War in 1845) when their officers had all been killed and their sergeants gallantly stepped in and saved the day. This was the excuse for a display of marching and counter-marching with band and drums when the Regiment's Colours were handed over to the sergeants for the day.

It was an impressive display and was followed by a very pleasant party in their Officers' Mess. I was delighted to meet again a number of officers whom I had known in the Wessex Brigade at Plymouth; and kept in touch with them in the following months as our paths often crossed on the sports field, at the Kowloon clubs or on formal occasions.

Christmas

The biggest social event of the Dorset year was of course Christmas. The holiday programme was tremendous. We converted the old Officers' Mess of the Middlesex Regiment into 'St Aldhelm's church', and on Christmas Eve held a carol service there run by Padre Dodds. Later that evening, the single officers were all invited out to dinner by the wives of our married men. I went into Kowloon as the guest of John and Jocelyn Reynolds who were charming hosts and entertained me generously in their delightful flat. They gave me a big Chinese meal, which was followed by more carol-singing on their balcony until 1 in the morning - to the horror of their Chinese neighbours.

After three hours sleep, the subalterns of D Company gave the troops "gunfire" when they woke in their Nissen huts in the lines on Christmas morning. The Sergeants and Sergeant-Majors took round cups of tea to the soldiers in bed, and I found myself following them round, handing out much-appreciated cigarettes as the officers' gift to every member of the company. They then sat down to a huge breakfast, and got up their appetite in a knock-out tournament on the football field, with a second carol service later in the morning.

The high-light of the day was the troops' Christmas dinner. Starting at 1 o'clock, it went on all afternoon with an excellent meal of traditional turkey and plum pudding cooked by the sergeants and served by the officers - though we were not very practised waiters. The cookhouse was gaily decorated and everyone enjoyed themselves with all the usual songs and toasts, but we officers were exhausted and glad to return to our own meal in mid-afternoon.

On Christmas evening, while the troops enjoyed a concert in the cookhouse, Brian Edwards and I were invited out by John and Maisie Drew who gave us a sumptuous meal in their long, low bungalow among the married quarters at Sek Kong. We listened to the Queen's first Christmas broadcast when she came on the air in Hong Kong late in the evening, and as it was so warm, the party continued out of doors chatting with the Drews' friendly neighbours long into the night.

Boxing Day saw the annual Officers v Sergeants football match. To the accompaniment of fire crackers and much boisterous shouting from the touchline, the officers lost by three goals to two. I had played little football since prep school and I was not in the least skilled; so I was put on the right wing out of harm's way. Even so, to my surprise, I nearly scored one goal, missing the net by a hair's breadth, and I proudly took part in several abortive attacking movements.

The officers were then entertained in the sergeants' mess, which was an even more exhausting exercise. It was not until the evening that the living-in officers were able to have their own celebrations, putting on dinner jackets and settling down to our own Christmas dinner which I, as Messing Officer, had purchased for them. The Compradore had prepared it excellently, including candles, brandy sauce, mince pies, crackers and nuts - and all the trimmings that I had been able to arrange.

The New Year

By contrast, the year end saw little celebration. I spent the afternoon playing rugger against the Gunners, and the evening in a big party of fellow Dorset officers at the Club. Everyone insisted on eating Chinese food which was not particularly well-prepared, and used chopsticks which I never found easy. After '*auld lang syne*' and a couple more drinks, the party broke up and I was able to share a taxi back to Camp.

The Mule Gymkhana was the highlight of the following day, having been postponed from Boxing Day because of heavy rain. There was a bar on the sports ground in a big NAAFI tent, and soldiers and officers let their hair down and laughed together. The racing provided endless amusement. The mules were the devils to ride, but most of us had a go. The jockeys dressed up in weird colours and few ever finished the course, but that hardly mattered. We then watched a series of imaginative and exotic races, such as jeeps driven backwards, obstacle motor-cycle races, races for old soldiers and many others, while each Company kept a number of side shows going during the afternoon.

Knocker's arrival

We made the coming of our new CO in January the excuse for two Dinner Nights. We had a rehearsal during the week preceding his arrival which was almost as much fun as the special Night on his arrival at the Camp. We were forty round the table with nine VIP guests including the Brigadier and the

Colonels of neighbouring regiments. Tim and Anne Ealand came out on the same boat as Knocker to rejoin the Battalion; so Tim was our guest that night as well, and I was delighted to see him again. Because of the number of guests, our batmen had been roped in to serve as waiters and did very well. The turkey was excellent, and the port flowed in plenty.

After the savoury, we sang with the Band long into the night all the old regimental songs that Knocker so loved, and we finished the evening off with a chaotic game of Billiards Fives which kept our guests happy until they slipped off into the night.

Exercise Grapeshot III

This was a Dinner Night with a difference, thought up by Knocker as a repeat of a similar exercise he had invented in a lull in the fighting in November 1944 when he had been CO of the 2nd Dorsets in Burma. He invited numerous guests, and arranged for us subalterns to entertain them with various silly skits and pantomimes; Gerald Blight was the Spirit of Fairyland; Douglas Jenks was Napoleon blown away with a whiff of grapeshot; and even the mules had their place in the show. Over seventy officers sat down to supper that night, and followed it with two hours of music and singing. It was a noisy affair; two tables were broken in the excitement, and our guests stayed a long time.

Formation Day

In late February, Knocker decided the Battalion should celebrate the 251st anniversary of the foundation of the regiment. The Brigadier took the salute at a march past with the Colours on our parade ground; and Padre Dodds officiated at a Drumhead Service to which wives and families were invited. The Padre read the Collect of the Dorset Regiment;

> "O Christ, Our Redeemer, the sure stronghold of each succeeding age; grant that we, who now bear arms in the Dorset Regiment may endure, as our fathers did before us, with steadfast courage. Lead us in every quarter of the earth; that we may not only honour and proclaim Thy name, but also serve to open a highway of Thy salvation for all mankind; through the same Jesus Christ, who now liveth and reigneth with the Father and Holy Spirit, one God, world without end."

The wives of the married officers took over the Officers' Mess and we ate a large curry, passed round the port and had a great party. I met several of those ladies whose company I had much enjoyed on the Empire Fowey, but of whom I had seen little while they were living in Kowloon a long way from Camp.

The Welch party

I was among a party of subalterns invited to a Guest Night in the Welch Regiment Officers Mess in January. We found them excellent hosts living in a luxurious and beautiful Mess with its own gardens and tennis court. We heard the full story how their regimental mascot, an unfortunate Welsh goat, had been painted green by a daring man from the Royal Ulster Rifles on St Patrick's Day. They had some fine mess silver and a first class dance band that played to us far into the night. We returned the compliment not long afterwards, sent the older members of the Mess to bed early and entertained their subalterns and others from all over the Brigade and kept the party going very cheerfully.

Naval Occasions

In mid-April, a group of us went with the CO in his Rover one morning to be the guests of HMS Unicorn for a day. We boarded the picket boat at Kowloon Steps, were soaked going out as it was a windy day but recovered as soon as we stepped on board, just remembering to salute their quarterdeck.

We were shown round the ship. It was a medium-sized aircraft carrier that had not been in action although it had often sailed in Korean waters. It had just come back from Kurie after taking a large party of soldiers from Hong Kong on a tour of South Korea and Japan. Its main job had been bringing planes up from Singapore to reinforce other carriers; and it was then on its way back to Singapore with a cargo of damaged planes for repair and refits. We were shown over each hangar, crossed the flight deck, and went up to the bridge to see the great number and variety of instruments required to sail the vast ship.

In due course we were taken down to the ward-room which was very luxurious and comfortable, and were entertained royally. When we eventually dragged ourselves away, I accompanied Ivor Ramsay in his private car in the pouring rain to visit our sick officers in the BMH to cheer them up before returning to Camp.

A couple of weeks later, several of us attended a big cocktail party on HMS Cossack in the harbour when once again my precious uniform was soaked returning in the picket boat. We repaid their hospitality in April when a party from the Unicorn and the Cossack, both coincidentally in harbour at the same time, came up to spend twenty-four hours or so at the Camp. While the sailors had a noisy sing-song at the NAAFI, we gave their officers an equally noisy Dinner Night in the Mess, put them up in our spare rooms, and took them the following morning on a tour of the frontier and up into the hills to view our defensive positions. Their visit ended with our Band beating the Retreat for them in a fine display.

The Queen's Birthday

On the morning of the new Queen's birthday, the powers that be decided we should fly the flag and demonstrate the British army's might to the inhabitants of Kowloon with a massive parade through the city. The authorities chose her real birthday, her first on the throne, in preference to the Official Birthday when she Trooped the Colour on Horseguards Parade at home.

Our Battalion rose at 5am and were off in a convoy of 3 ton lorries by 6.30 that morning to find our place in the long line of marching troops and vehicles. With our band behind us in smart white jackets playing all the regimental tunes, and with the imposing figure of Knocker White at our head, each company marched with fixed bayonets six abreast, the width of the Kowloon carriageways. The officers led each company, wearing freshly-laundered and starched 'olive green' uniforms and carrying gleaming swords resting on our shoulders. We marched well, even though the Band was too far away for my company to hear the drum beats. The long column included a squadron of tanks, a bevy of personnel carriers, and a procession of foot-soldiers drawn from every battalion in the Colony. It must have been an impressive display.

The Chinese populace turned out in some numbers to watch us. They lined the broad roads ten deep; and I think we were all impressed with their interest if not their enthusiasm. The Governor took the salute on a dais opposite the United Services Club, and looked a tremendous figure in his full dress and cocked hat with its plume of feathers.

Government House

In late April, several of us were invited to a Garden Party at Government House in Victoria on the Island. We dressed up in our best white 'No. 3' uniforms and were driven up to the mighty front doors in style. It was a hot afternoon when Gerald Blight and I arrived and strolled out into the garden across a long hall, past a gracious drawing room and a panelled dining room, and among priceless Chinese urns and vases. While the garden was nothing much - merely a strip of lawn along the front of the mansion - the view was superb, for we could look out over the harbour full of ships, and across to Kowloon with the mountains of the New Territories beyond.

The Dorset band played in the background as we mingled with a very smart crowd including numerous service officers and their wives in all their finery. Neither the Governor nor Lady Grantham were tall people; she wore a very wide flowery hat and all we could see of her was its broad brim floating gently among her guests - a bit like a butterfly going from one colourful flower to the next. So we sipped our tea and munched some of their sandwiches and

April 1953. Hong Kong, In No 3 dress for the Government House garden party.

much enjoyed the occasion. Afterwards, Gerald and I slipped away to have our pictures wearing 'No 3 dress' taken by a photographer in the Mayfair Studio in Kowloon.

Norset Day

This day was celebrated whenever the Dorset and Royal Norfolk Regiments were stationed within reach of each other. They had combined as one unit to fight the Turks at Kut al Amara in 1915 and sought every opportunity to recall their temporary union. As they were both stationed in Hong Kong in 1953, it was decided to hold a Norset parade on the ninth anniversary of the capture of the District Commissioner's Bungalow spur at Kohima (which was always a day of celebration for the Dorset Regiment, especially in Knocker's calendar).

Thus 13th May was the occasion for a grand joint parade to which were invited the Governor, the naval Commodore, the GOC and all the military bigwigs and their spouses. The Dorset officers spent the previous night until 1 o'clock man-handling furniture in the mess and marquees outside which we carpeted and stocked with bars. We manufactured a most excellent cocktail and consumed large quantities in order to make sure it was suitable for HE; and I fear some of us were jaded before the day started.

By 10.30am, all officers and soldiers were in their Sunday best, and were busy on the parade ground along with a large number of Norfolks. As we were celebrating the battles our predecessors had fought together, we were both hosts, although the parade took place on the Dorset parade ground. We had rows of chairs for spectators and a 'Royal Box' for the Governor and his escort, and the square looked very smart under new tar. It was a very warm day but fortunately overcast. We received two hundred guests, the men in white or drill uniforms, and their wives in sun hats and parasols to ward off the sun. The Commodore arrived by helicopter which added tone to the proceedings. It was a simple parade, a salute, an inspection, speeches from both Colonels, a show by the Bands and Drums of the Regiments (marred just a little by three men fainting from heat and one Norfolk drummer knocking off his hat with his drum-stick), a march-past and the anthem.

Then we took HE and our guests up to the Mess which I imagine had never been so full before. In the middle, a sharp, heavy shower drove everybody from the 'gardens' into the tents, and we were very squashed when we gave them the cocktail and a good buffet lunch. Then we had a very special photograph taken to commemorate the day, all Norfolk and all Dorset officers in a group with HE in the centre.

We went back into the Mess and continued to amuse our guests who insisted on staying considerably longer than expected. As soon as the last ones had drifted away, the hosts gathered in the dining room and seized some of the buffet which we had not been able to consume earlier while looking after our visitors. Then we rushed to our rooms, stripped off Sam Browne and white jacket - which was by then no more than a stained, bedraggled rag - put on some comfortable civilian clothes, and ran down to our playing fields. Here the second half of the programme was in full swing - Norfolk v Dorset sports; cricket which was very entertaining and an easy win to us; football which was won 9 - 1 by our 'crack' team; and various other games. We had a delightful tea on the pitch and were sorry to have to leave in order to get ready for the third part of the proceedings - the evening.

This time the Dorsets were entertained by the Norfolks at their Camp. We got into fresh mess kit and left in a fleet of land-rovers and lorries - a lot of troops went out too. First we were invited to watch the combined bands beat Retreat, which we did in another heavy downpour. We then adjourned to their officers' mess for drinks, a buffet supper and an impromptu dance with their dance-band in their ante-room. After a while, some of us Dorsets were invited to their Sergeants' mess. The Sergeants wore white mess jackets and bow ties and looked considerably smarter than most officers until one or two exceeded their normal drinking capacity. Back in the officers' mess the party continued, dancing to a radiogram after the band was packed off to bed. We crawled home very late but well satisfied with successful celebrations.

My Twenty-first birthday

28th May was a normal day in the Camp. I opened my birthday presents - Margaret, Roger and Robin[1] sent me the book *"A Pattern of Islands"* by Arthur Grimble, which was my first introduction to the Colonial Service; Liz gave me a Coronation Loving Cup which I have been proud to display on my mantelpiece

---
1   Robin is the eldest son of my sister Margaret, born in August 1952.

ever since; my kind aunts, my father's partners and my father sent me generous cheques. In the evening, there was a routine Dinner Night with a delightful dinner in a very full mess, and we enjoyed a pleasant evening sitting outside on our terrace listening to the Band. When everyone was relaxed I smoked a big cigar which made me feel slightly ill, told them it was my birthday and bought a large round of drinks - as was the custom. They congratulated me, drank their tipple and sloped off to bed.

Disappointed somehow at the lack of celebration, I was lonely and acutely homesick that evening; I was full of energy too. If I could not celebrate with my family, I wanted to do something different and special by which to remember the occasion. When everyone had gone to bed, I slipped out of the back of the Mess on my own and climbed to the top of Badge Hill. It was pitch dark and it was a foolish thing to do in evening dress. All I could show for it was a pair of ruined slippers.

That night, a thousand miles away in Korea, the Chinese launched wave after wave of savage attacks against the Duke of Wellington's Regiment and the King's Regiment on a feature known as 'The Hook'. Our soldiers fought with great courage in a fierce and desperate battle under constant heavy artillery bombardment. The hill was held and both battalions distinguished themselves despite severe casualties.

The Coronation

On Sunday, 31st May we celebrated the Coronation. We had a Brigade Church Parade in the morning followed by a Fair and Gymkhana on the model of the successful event on New Year's Day. Despite very wet weather, tents were put up on the sports field, the wives and families came out from Hong Kong, the Band played and the NAAFI ran a tea tent and bar. Each Company organised a side show, including a boxing booth, a darts competition, weight-lifting and a .22 miniature rifle range. D Company ran a coconut shy, charging fifty cents for three balls and made $150. Peter Pearmain, who had recently joined the Company, had spent the previous night searching the dirtiest markets and docks of Kowloon for the coconuts.

The races were much the same as those that had taken place at the New Year and were still the greatest fun. Bill Heald was at the microphone; Steve Elvery was the starter, and the two of them entertained us all afternoon. The jockeys wore their rugger or hockey jerseys and gave us some good runs despite the heavy going. Brian Hawkins who had joined A Company distinguished himself by his control of the beast and led the field with panache. Most of the jockeys fell off to the delight of the children, but as it was so wet, no-one was much hurt - merely covered in mud. We gave the wives and other guests a duck curry for lunch in the Mess; and we all went down to the NAAFI in the evening for a buffet supper followed by a cheerful sing-song and entertainment by the Band.

The following Tuesday, the day of the Coronation itself back in London, was heralded by a massive thunderstorm and lightening overhead. The Brigade assembled on our parade ground and marched past General Cruddas with due ceremony. We gave the General Salute followed by a Royal Salute and a mighty three cheers for the Queen. The officers then fell out and met in a tent on the field, to drink a toast to the Queen in NAAFI Champagne, and that was that. I was confined to barracks as the Orderly Officer, but I heard snatches of the broadcast of the ceremony on Douglas Jenks' wireless through the partition wall.

A couple of weeks later, we were on parade again, for the Brigadier to present Coronation Medals to the CO, the Quarter-Master, the RSM, the Band Master and three or four others. That was altogether a happier occasion, although earlier that morning the CO decided the officers were bad at sword drill and should have some practice. We were bad; but there were more important things to do on a Saturday morning than sword drill.

The Colonel-in-Chief

Very soon afterwards, the Colonel heard that Princess Marina, the Duchess of Kent, had been appointed by the Queen to be Colonel-in-Chief of the Dorset Regiment. We were mustered in a hollow square around a hallowed piece of the regimental silver known as the 'Duke of Kent's Cup'. Knocker read out the Proclamation of the Princess' appointment; we gave her three cheers; the cup was then placed on the saluting base and we marched past it in column of threes. In the Mess we had a Dinner Night and, for the first time, had the opportunity of drinking the Duchess' health.

The Plassey dance

My last Battalion party was the Plassey Dance at the Kowloon Cricket Club. After an absurdly expensive evening meal at the Peninsula Hotel, a group of us Dorset officers went on to the Club and passed two and a half hours of duty drinking among our NCOs and soldiers.

The D Company men were drinking deep in a room by themselves off the dance hall, and at some expense I bought them all another round, and used the occasion as a chance to talk to the NCOs about their families and personal affairs. The CO made a cheerful speech about the Duchess of Kent; and then we trundled home in a convoy of land-rovers and three tonners reaching Camp in the early morning.

The bright lights

All of us in the Camp used to try to go down to Kowloon and Hong Kong Island most weekends for two reasons - to enjoy the shops, the restaurants and the bright lights, or alternatively, as soon as it grew hot, to have a swim.

The trouble was that the roads were so poor, and the buses and trains so crowded that the journey to Kowloon and back was never easy and often downright unpleasant. The Battalion ran a bus during the week to bring in to Camp the married NCOs and Warrant Officers who lived in Kowloon, while the married officers tended to do the trip in their own cars, but they all found it a tedious and wearying journey. Occasionally too it was dangerous; one Sunday in June, a party of married officers and their wives who were expected at a service in St Aldhelm's Church in the Camp limped in very late with their smart uniforms and the ladies' dresses covered from head to foot in thick, sticky mud. Their Morris Oxford had tried to overtake the battalion bus, caught it a glancing blow, and bounced off it into a paddy field where rice was growing in a foot of water.

The battalion transport left Kowloon at 8am each weekday morning and returned from the Camp to the city at 6pm; trucks went to and fro at weekends, but generally on duty trips and seldom at times convenient for those of us wanting an evening out. Sometimes a special truck would be going in, but it would generally be heavily overloaded, emit clouds of exhaust fumes and offer a very uncomfortable ride as it jolted and bounced along the coast road. Often

I wished I had brought out my motor cycle from Dorchester. Though low-powered, it would have given me much greater freedom on free weekends and holidays.

There was one consolation on the coast road. Nine miles out from Kowloon, where the road ran down to the sea, was a little fishing village called Sha Tin; and, as one entered the village on the drive back to Camp after an afternoon in the bright lights, one came to a rough and ready restaurant built on stilts over the sands looking across the bay. *The Sha Tin Dairy Farm Restaurant* offered us 'Green Spots' at 40 cents (our most popular soft drink), or cold beers for $1.50 and a ham and eggs for $3. This is what the Restaurant said about itself.

> *"Besides the best food, liquor and petrol services we provide; the beauty, attractions and tranquillity of our site are matchless and unique. This is the nearest modern suburban restaurant most easily accessible by train, bus, bike and motor car.*
>
> *This is the only place you can watch and feel a roaring train as you eat. Occasionally you will be thrilled by shooting Vampires smacking out of the blue. You'll witness, together with hundreds of ducks, the fast and eternal celestial changes of the Tide four times a day.*
>
> *Your junior folk may enjoy fishing, fording, boating, ferrying, crabbing, clamming, or simply playing around the shallow mangroves. This is the place you'll enjoy most! Please come again and save a trip to Miami or Geneva."*

Buses went from Fan Ling into Kowloon with some frequency, but their timing was erratic and destination uncertain. Even if one could catch one going in the right direction at roughly the right time, it tended to be heavily overloaded with local folk, their belongings in massive wicker baskets and their livestock of various smelly sorts.

In preference to the bus, when there was no military transport, we used the train to Kowloon. I enjoyed it and found it useful at times, even though the railway station at Fan Ling was three miles from the Camp. Tricycle rickshaws at the station used to plague us to carry us back to Camp in style for a dollar or so, but we often preferred to walk home. The road from the station was fascinating. On either side stood Chinese fruit and vegetable stalls, eating houses, and numerous shacks, lit after dark in a yellow glow by paraffin lamps on rickety tables. Men sat at these tables eating rice from little decorated bowls with chopsticks, and playing cards or Mah Jong far into the night. We used to tramp home, tired and loaded with shopping, to the accompaniment of their tinky-tonk music, the hissing lamps, the nasal chatter of the card players and the click-clack of the Mah Jong tiles.

The snag was that the last train left Kowloon station at 10.45pm. On numerous occasions, a group of us missed it after a good night out and had to persuade a taxi to take us back to Camp at two or three o'clock in the morning. The driver charged anything from $25 to $30 for the trip, which was hugely expensive, but we had no choice if we were to be on duty in Camp the following morning.

Swimming

Our nearest bathing beach was at Castle Peak, and several of us hitched a lift to go down there on the first Sunday after our arrival at San Wai. We found a long sandy beach and enjoyed excellent swimming among the enormous rocks scattered along its length. We seldom went back however, partly because it became too cold to think of swimming for the following four months, and partly because as it grew warmer again, other beaches elsewhere seemed more inviting. We resumed swimming again at Easter 1953, when we dug our bathing trunks out from the bottom of our suitcases and found the sea a delightful escape from the daily grind at the Camp. For my first bathe of the year, when the sea was warming up, Tim and Anne Ealand took me to a secluded beach just beyond Castle Peak. Thereafter we all escaped as often as possible to go swimming.

The soldiers sought out beaches all round the peninsula and on the island. We tried the swimming at Taipo on the north shore which was probably the closest to the Camp though still quite a haul, but it was noisy and messy as it was close to the village and fish market. Sek Kong to the south was also within reach and each battalion was given the opportunity to enjoy its facilities in turns, but the more distant beaches were the more secluded, bigger and better. Clearwater Bay was much farther away but had broad sparkling sands. The best beaches were undoubtedly on the north side of the Island. Big Wave Bay was a favourite, but inaccessible. Of them all, most of us preferred Repulse Bay which I first explored with my A Company Platoon in the Battalion bus. It was set amid beautiful countryside, under the attractive hills that stretched across the island; we found it ideal in every respect, at least on weekdays when no one else was around, and went back there whenever we could.

The United Services Recreation Club

When time allowed at weekends, we officers fled to the swimming pool at the USRC. Their bath was open all day until 6pm for children, and thereafter reserved for adults with a bar alongside, and we could swim and drink and swim and drink all night if we wished.

Just about every Dorset officer paid the small subscription to become a member of the Club. In addition to the pool, it offered a dining room, a comfortable lounge with wicker chairs and English newspapers, a library and an outdoor cinema in dry weather. The cloakrooms were handy and useful for changing one's clothes, for example from sports gear into evening dress, if one was going out in the evening.

One signed chits for everything and received a monthly bill. The food was only mediocre - indeed it put me off Chinese food for ever - but the big indoor bar was a good spot for meeting people. You could always find a few Dorset officers having a drink there on a weekend evening, and it was a very handy rendezvous. On my first weekend, I met the only other Old Shirburnian in the Colony, David Fayle, my School House contemporary, then in an artillery regiment. Later on, it was there I bumped into two other OS when they were passing through; a chap named Peplow on his way to Korea, and Waugh, of School House who was a midshipman on a naval ship in harbour.

Kowloon

The city was teeming with people at all times and consisted of mile upon mile of blocks of high rise flats. There were also good gift and clothing shops, cinemas and restaurants of all sorts, fortunately within walking distance of each other. To move around, it was easy and cheap to hire a rickshaw but those who pulled me never seemed to know their way and I preferred a taxi.

On our first Sunday in the town, we made a point of calling on the popular tailor known as Savalanis. We visited him regularly thereafter for he made passable suits to measure - better than Au Wai Lam at the camp - and he was able to equip us with exotic clothing like silk shirts, embroidered dressing gowns and shark-skin dinner jackets. He also cashed our cheques, which was very convenient because the Hong Kong and Shanghai Bank was open for only a few hours each weekday, and their staff were off-hand, inefficient and unhelpful.

We also found two or three good photographic shops to develop our films, and we patronised several passable restaurants. One was Russian called *Tchachenko* where we were served enormous steaks for very little. We were there on the night Stalin died and were amused to note that the staff was not in the least downcast or sad at his passing.

The Peninsula Hotel

This hotel opposite the docks was very grand in the old colonial style. Some of the married officers had rooms there; and we sometimes called in to relax in comfortable air-conditioned surroundings in their spacious lounge, while in their stylish dining room we could eat well in a civilised atmosphere. The food was of a high standard at a price to match; it was at the hotel that for the first time in my life I was served with frozen food - in this case strawberries from Japan.

I went to a big dance at the Pen in May. It was organised by a Mrs Robertson, a prosperous and hospitable American lady, for the benefit of young army officers and the young ladies of Hong Kong. She held a series of dances during the winter, and Gerald Blight, then the General's ADC, gave me a ticket for the last one before the summer. I took a partner, joined a big party, and thoroughly enjoyed the evening though it was horribly expensive, and I crawled back to camp in my DJ at 2.30am.

The Flicks

We often went for relaxation to the Kowloon cinemas. They were dirty and smelly downstairs but luxurious in the good seats upstairs, and they had the great advantage of being air-conditioned. A film proved a very a good way to cool down on a Saturday evening, and we frequently took refuge in a cinema to watch a film as the weather grew warmer.

The cinemas generally showed the latest Hollywood films. I saw with my friends films like, *"Quo Vadis"* which lasted over three hours, *"The Snows of Kilimanjaro"* with Gregory Peck, *"Cyrano de Bergerac"* with Jose Ferrer, and

"*Against all Flags*" with Erroll Flynn and Maureen O'Hara. We also saw a few good British films including the excellent "*The Desert Rats*" with James Mason. At the Alhambra Cinema in Kowloon, I saw my first horror film which was also my first three D film called "*The House of Wax*" - and I decided neither experience was worth repeating.

Hong Kong Island

The romantic harbour lying between Kowloon and Victoria was always busy with junks, sampans and craft of every shape and size passing to and fro. While we were there, the spacious bay generally also contained a selection of merchantmen and British naval craft on their way to and from Korean waters. It was a magnificent sight when one of the aircraft carriers like HMS Glory or HMS Cossack was in port.

On our first Sunday in Kowloon I tried out the Star Ferry which for a mere 20 cents carried one across the harbour to the terminal in Victoria. I always enjoyed the short journey, despite the crowds and scrum but one had to allow lots of time. Once on the Island it was a delight to explore the busy, noisy and malodorous shopping streets that criss-crossed the lower levels of the city. We admired the curios, ivory and jade objects in the shop-windows and paid visits to some of the many little restaurants tucked away in the side streets. At Jimmy's Kitchen, we could have a good meal for $15; it seemed a lot in those days but was well worth the expense. The Cock and Pullet was another pleasant place for a supper. At The Gloucester Lounge, we could sit back in an easy chair in air-conditioned splendour and have a light lunch and a refreshing milk-shake.

A special pleasure was my visit to the Victoria home of a prosperous business man, Mr Hill, who was a friend of Mrs Maas, the mother of James, who had been in School House with me. Mr Hill lived in a beautiful house with elegant furniture and some striking chinoiserie. His big windows looked out to sea over Repulse Bay and across to the scattered islands in the distance. I was impressed by his three servants and big Chrysler car, and I was enthralled by his conversation and his many stories of Hong Kong and the Chinese people whom he knew well. I was sorry to have to leave to catch the last train that evening, and regret I was never able to repeat my visit because it so happened he was returning to the UK for a spell of leave.

Two or three of us took time to call at the magnificent Royal Hong Kong Yacht Club. I signed in and enquired arrangements for hiring sailing dinghies, but regrettably never had time to sail there. I was able to stay at the Yacht Club on two or three occasions, however, and found it very useful when required to spend a night on the island in order to attend athletic matches over there.

Gerald Blight and I visited both the Hong Kong Club and the beautiful Cricket Club with its neat square of green in the midst of the skyscrapers. We had a look too at the race course at Happy Valley, but once again I regretted I was never able to follow up these calls because we had only brief opportunities to cross to the Island.

More memorable was the occasion when I had my haircut in Victoria. We had learned that the GOC insisted on a neat head on his officers and all rushed off to the barbers a day or two before his formal annual inspection. For my special haircut I was taken to a little place at the back of the old town and had a delightful experience. The young man who did the job gave me a wonderfully relaxing scalp and neck massage, which revived me and was well worth the extra dollar. I then returned to the USRC to spend the afternoon lounging by the Club's pool and soaking up the sun.

My happiest evening on the Island was however on the eve of the Coronation. I was Orderly Officer on the big day itself, so went in with Peter Boultbee, the MO, to see the sights the preceding afternoon. Peter and I were keen to see the Dragon Procession that was scheduled to pass through Victoria - the dragon was reputed to be 200 yards long and to be followed by lions and a menagerie of other beasts. Sadly we never saw them, for the crowds were so closely packed at the ferry terminal that we had great difficulty in disembarking and found access to the processional route quite impenetrable.

We gave up and went our separate ways; and I went up the Peak Railway instead. The tramway was mildly alarming but the views in all directions from the top were magnificent. I stayed on the summit until well after dark when I had the finest view of all, listening to the preparations for the ceremony on wirelesses through the windows of the big houses up there. The illuminations on a normal night were very fine, and over the period of the Coronation, they were especially beautiful. Braziers burned along the shore, while all the huge buildings and skyscrapers on both sides of the water were outlined in coloured

116 Bullshit Baffles Brains

Hong Kong Island. The Eve of the Coronation, June 1st, 1953. The impenetrable crowd watching the Dragon Procession.

lights which were reflected in the sea. The ships in the harbour were dressed overall and brilliantly lit from stem to stern. That was a special and unique experience.

When I went back over the ferry I was invited in to Reggie Hill's rooms in the Peninsula Hotel. Other Dorset officers drifted in, and we were entertained with beer from a collection of bottles cooling in his bath and piles of sandwiches provided by the management. From Reggie and Doris' balcony we watched the lights and the firework display. At the same time over their wireless, we heard Richard Dimbleby's reports of the procession in London and the crowning in Westminster Abbey. At 10.50pm, we switched the wireless on to hear the mighty roar of the crowd as the anointed Queen came out of the Abbey in her Coronation robes.

Sport

On the sports fields we played football, hockey and rugger. I chose my usual position on the rugger field on the left wing and played for the Battalion in the Army Knock-out Competition. We had regular practices before our first match which was a rough but exciting game against the Wiltshires that we won convincingly. We lost the following week, however, when playing on the Kowloon Police ground against the 45th Field Regiment R.A. who were much stronger than us.

I took part in several inter-company hockey games and in light-hearted matches between the officers and the sergeants which proved challenging battles. I found myself acting as referee in some of the company games which was just as enjoyable as playing in the games. Football was played enthusiastically throughout the Camp and was highly competitive, but I had even less skill with my feet than with my hands and played only when press-ganged in the Boxing Day match between officers and sergeants.

There were masses of opportunities for other sport at San Wai during the cooler months. On a new squash court built by the Middlesex Regiment behind the Camp, I played a certain amount and relished the exercise though was regularly beaten.

A number of our men were practised and powerful boxers that took on other battalions and did well. Our boxing team took on the RUR on one special occasion in a bloodthirsty and high class match. The entire Ulster and Dorset Battalions gathered round the ring on our sports ground to cheer their men. It was an exciting afternoon; the crowd's numbers and noise was just as exhilarating as the boxing, which the Irish won by six fights to four.

The Battalion Inter-company Athletics Meeting

I was made responsible for sorting out D Company's team for the Battalion's athletics match at the New Year. We did a limited amount of practising on the track before Christmas, but when the day came, fielded a strong team for all the usual track and field events. We faced the other companies on the grass track of the sports ground below the Camp in the presence of plenty of supporters who were well fortified at the NAAFI bar.

It was my first exposure to such a competition, and I was gratified to find my Company came in fourth overall. We learned a lot about competitive racing, even though we came away with few awards. My own performance pleased me too as I did well on behalf of the Company in the 880 yards.

The Battalion Individual Championships

I was gaining fitness and confidence all the time, and trained hard for our individual championships. We took over a good cinder track in Kowloon where a big crowd of soldiers and families came down to cheer us on, despite depressing weather. I entered for both the 440 yards and 880 yards. I survived the heats with no trouble. In the half mile final, in a big field, Cpl Freeth and I emerged in front. He had longer legs than I but was newly out of hospital after the 'quad' accident. It was a horribly close finish, but I was just able to reach the tape ahead of him (in 2mins 17.1 seconds!) I then ran in the quarter mile final and came in second behind Bob Reep. I came away with a little cup and a shield.

In mid-November I took over the organisation of the Battalion's long-distance running. I organised team training and set up and ran in several cross-country runs. We challenged the RUR to a race over on a course through the hills around our camps. It was the Dorset's first experience of competitive racing that year, and we found we were up against some strong runners, and lost dismally.

I then joined the Battalion's Athletic Team and helped to arrange a thorough training programme and a series of athletics matches within the Battalion. We did not do well in the preliminary trials in early December, for we had had no time to sort ourselves out or to train, but we soon put that right. I started to train seriously for the quarter and half mile, and found myself pulling my weight as a member of the team. We continued to train and run throughout the colder months and I ran for the Battalion in several athletics matches at weekends. We were led by Bob Reep who had the long legs of a fine hurdler, while Gerald Blight with his slim build was outstanding as a high jumper.

We had a second match with the RUR in an invitation event on our ground. We were gratified and perhaps surprised to find we could beat them at the shorter distances. I ran in the half mile, did well in the heats and came in second in the final - and should have done better. Our 440x relay team also did well, and I overtook my opponent even though he started some way ahead of me. It was thus our Battalion took their revenge for the beating we had received at the hands of their boxing team.

The Brigade Athletics Meeting

The Brigade match took place in one of the busiest parts of Kowloon during three days of bedlam. It was the weekend of the Chinese New Year; not only was there a reign of terror in the Mess while our batmen took over from the Chinese cooks and Mess staff who were on holiday, there was also noisy chaos in Kowloon all round the ground where we were racing. The shops were shut; the streets were thronged with people; many roads were impassable with the crowds; and the noise of fire crackers and squibs was continuous and immensely off-putting.

We knew we could beat the RUR at short distances, but were uncertain of our overall strength. At the Brigade meeting, however, our team confronted and resoundingly defeated the determined opposition of both the RUR and the Welch Regiment. I ran in the 440 and 880 yards relay races. In the 4 x 880 relay I ran the first leg and held my position, but the third of our runners muddled handing over the baton and we could only manage second place at the finishing line.

The 4 x 440 relay was the last event of the day. I was very nervous beforehand, somewhat intimidated by the big crowd cheering us on. We had by then established a clear lead over the other teams however, so the pressure was off, and when it came to the point I thoroughly enjoyed a good tough race. I ran rather better than I had earlier in the day, and was ahead of the others when I handed the baton over to Klaus Marx. He took the lead; we won the race easily and collected little silver cups for our pains. The Dorsets thus completed the rout of both the Ulstermen and the Welshmen and won the 27 Brigade competition.

The Land Forces Championships

We then had two weeks in which to prepare for the Hong Kong all-Army meeting. This was a four day event, of which the first half comprised individual entries; and the second half consisted of team events when the Dorsets challenged the winners of the other Brigade's meeting, and the best of the Gunners and the Tanks.

The Athletics Team was not allowed to go on a major six-day Battalion Exercise in the hills known as *'Exercise Mercara'*. I was bitterly disappointed at the prospect of missing this important training scheme and grumbled noisily, but Knocker took the right decision. I spent the morning before their departure at the Mule Lines idly watching the beasts being loaded with the battalion's heavy equipment - a task requiring skill and enormous patience. I then waved goodbye to John Drew and D Company as they set off on foot for the hills. The temperature shot up between ten and fifteen degrees at the very moment the Battalion left the Camp at the start of the Exercise. As a result the men had a very rough time and we athletes were better out of it. During the hour it took the seven hundred soldiers to reach their positions in the hills, around eighty dropped out with heat exhaustion - mostly the Fusiliers who had not had time to get acclimatised. Moreover, the mules were recalcitrant in the heat, the wirelesses failed to work down the long column, and the last men straggled into their places three hours behind schedule and long after dark.

The athletes trained hard in those last few days and went down to the track at Boundary Street in Kowloon for the first day of the Championship with high hopes. The first day of individual competition consisted mainly of 'field' events, and the heats of the 'track' events. I went in for the half mile race, ran well in the preliminary heats on the first day and qualified easily for the final which took place on the second day. I was then up against the army's best and came only fourth four or five seconds behind the winner who ran beautifully in 2 minutes 8 seconds. I enjoyed the race, however, and the several Dorsets on the track in Kowloon did well and had a good time supporting and encouraging each other.

I had no running to do on the third day of championship when the short distance track and more field events took place, and by the time I arrived at the sports field, we were already doing well, having won the 4 x 120 hurdles, and the 4 x 220 yards relay. I spent the afternoon looking after the kit of the athletes taking part, and cheering them on. We won the shot-put and the discus, but our most serious challenger, the 45 Field Regiment won the pole vault, and the Wiltshires won the 3 mile team race. By the end of the day we were just ahead of the Gunners on points and eager to complete the conquest of our opponents when the rain poured down and the final day of the competition was postponed for a week.

Our frustration increased at being unable to rejoin the battalion in the hills for the final part of the Exercise, but we kept in trim waiting for the rain to stop and the ground to dry up. Better still, the delay gave the Battalion time to complete their Exercise and pile into buses to give us support. A crowd of over four hundred of our regiment came along including many of the wives and children of our officers who gave us lots of noisy encouragement. Knocker was everywhere, giving us all lots of good cheer and advice. Whether because of their vociferous encouragement or not, when the match was resumed, we walked away with the Championship, coming first or second in every event.

In the 880 yards relay, Cpl Freeth who was normally our last string was slightly injured so he took the first leg and they put me in his place. Sadly one of the earlier Dorset runners muffed his hand-over and the race was already lost by the time the baton was in my hands. I drew away from the Wiltshire man who started just behind me and finished a comfortable second. After that race, we never looked back as a team, winning almost all the throwing and track events. We were first in the 4 x100 yards relays, thanks to Cpl Crane, the CO's batman; and our team stuck together to achieve a gratifying victory in the 1 mile team race. Gerald Blight and Brian Edwards won the high jump easily; two of our young Fusilier reinforcements took the long jump for us; two hefty Dorset sergeants won the javelin. The last race of the day was the 4 x 440 yards relay in which I ran as the first string. I got away well and was only a moment or two behind the leader when I passed the baton to Klaus Marx. He took the lead and the third and fourth strings forged ahead and had no difficulty in winning. The Regimental Journal paid us a slightly back-handed compliment.

> "The 4 x440 yards relay provided a final thrill. At the beginning of the meeting we were extremely dubious about the possibilities of our track event runners. The quarter mile team finally proved our fears to be groundless. 2/Lieut. Eberlie ran a great race to hold his own and hand over to 2 /Lieut. Marx who gained a lead for Cpl Knight who was able to improve on this for the benefit of Lieut. Reep who ran a sound 'Captain's' race to win by many yards from his nearest opponent."

The Dorsets thus became the Land Forces champions for 1953. Knocker was *'chuffed to bits'* as my diary put it, and of course the Battalion was cock-a-hoop. The prize-giving was tedious and slow but I added a little medal and a nice cup to my collection.

The 440 relay at the Championship. Here I am passing the baton to Klaus Marx.

After that exertion, I felt grim and found myself "fair done up" according to my batman. Instead of joining the others in celebrating, I went back to the Club, took some aspirin and went to sleep in a big arm-chair all the way through an Erroll Flynn film, and in the taxi going home. We had a small gathering the following morning in the Corporals' Club when Knocker said some very nice things about the team effort and a group photograph was taken with a long line of cups at our feet. We then proceeded to drink a potent mixture of rum and beer out of the Challenge Cup that had been presented us and celebrated our success.

The Colony AAA Championships

A couple of weeks later, our Team took part in a meeting at the Hong Kong Athletic Club at the South China sports ground beyond the Tiger Balm Pagoda. It was refreshingly non-military, but we had lost several of our key men who had been selected to represent the Regiment at the Coronation Parade in London. They had already left for home on the troopship, the SS Asturias. Moreover most of us had given up our strict training programme, as a result Dorset men did not do well. Indeed we failed to win any event; we were largely spectators, watching a walking race, pitying those who ran the 10,000 metres in the intense heat, and ending by exchanging banners with the other teams. Finally in early May, some of us ran in a civilian event on the RAF Sports Ground beyond Kai Tak airport. None of my fellow Dorset athletes nor I distinguished ourselves. The Chinese competitors showed us up. I was fourth out of five runners in the 800 metre race. That was the end of my running career.

Farewells

My time came to return home, and amid the chaos of Exercise Teacup, Bill Heald, Ross Moylan, Dick Campbell and I were all posted to Y Company to return to the UK on the Empire Clyde sailing from Hong Kong on July 4th. Bill Heald was on his way home to the Staff College; we three subalterns were returning to civilian life. Knocker generously made us the guests of the Mess at a farewell Dinner Night two nights before we left the Battalion. I sat on his right hand and found him charming. The Mess silver had been packed away in the mobilisation exercise, but the silver port carriage had been specially unpacked for the occasion, and the Band played in the ante-room as usual.

After a good meal, the speeches included a light and witty farewell by Ivor Ramsay on behalf of the Mess to those about to depart, and a friendly and up-beat response by Bill Heald. We drank three toasts, *"The Queen"*, *"The Duchess of Kent"*, and *"Those about to depart"*. The Band Master, Mr Plant was invited in and given a chair between the CO and me, and I complimented him - I hope gracefully. I was asked to choose a song for the Band to play; and the three of us who were leaving were required to sing a verse each of the *"The Farmer's Boy"*. Then the serious singing started; the Band played *"Buttercup Joe"* for me and finally *"Auld Lang Syne"*. Ivor sang us a little song of his own composition that summed up the occasion.

"When the Chinese land on Hong Kong strand,
Then the Dorsets, they will make them stand,
With a tin of Brasso in each hand.
Oh! The bullshit baffles brains.
When at last we reach Korea, the enemy will flee in fear,
For our green hose-tops will appear.
Oh! The bullshit baffles brains.
The wars were won oftentimes by cavalry charges and thin red lines,
But we win ours by painting signs.
Oh! The bullshit baffles brains."

There followed the usual singing to the Band and the customary violent hicockalorum and cock-fighting long into the night. Bill dashed back to Kowloon to finish packing up his flat with his wife and small son. For myself, I recalled little of the night though I know I broke a glass and was rather unsteady when finally I fell into bed under the mosquito net about 2am.

I was up again at 5am to pack my two tin trunks with the help of Long, my faithful batman. I spent the rest of the morning saying goodbye to the NCOs and soldiers in D Company, made a confused speech and was gratified when they gave me a round of applause. Then I put my foot in it, trying to persuade the Company Sergeant Major to transfer Long to work in the Officers' Mess which he badly wanted. I said the wrong thing and - to my consternation - left the CSM very angry. I was too confused to do anything but stutter, but I wrote to him from the boat to apologise as soon as I had the chance. Much later I received a warm and courteous reply greatly to my relief. I said my goodbyes to the NCOs and finally my fellow officers before boarding a truck with the others who were sailing with me.

At Kowloon I went aboard the Clyde and found my cabin, and then remembered to my horror that I had forgotten Bill Heald's trunk that he had asked me to pick up from the Mess, and I disembarked in a panic to the public phone box to ring through for it. The line was out of order which served to increase my panic. My relief was all the greater when, on clambering back on board I found Knocker, John and Marie Archer, and John and Jocelyn Reynolds who had all come down to see us off, bringing with them everything I had left behind. They stayed to have a final drink with Bill and his wife and the three of us subalterns, and I think we all much appreciated their gesture.

The "Empire Clyde"

Our boat was supposed to be comfortable, small and select, but it did not live up to its reputation. The food was *a la* Lyons Corner House at Marble Arch. It was good and solid, but not really up to much, and at times quite awful. The bar was good but the service slow, though I did little drinking, because I had run out of money. The cabin was hot and horribly smelly - we always knew what to expect for the next meal. When the average temperature below decks was 90 degrees, in our cabin it reached 100 degrees. As often as possible we slept on deck. I adapted my body to the planking of the deck-tennis court and the benches round it, which were comparatively comfortable; but none of us ever had a full night's sleep up there because a chilling head-wind rose in the early hours of the morning and the Scottish crew swabbed down the decks with hoses before the sun rose.

The South China Sea was peaceful as we sailed south. We paused at Singapore and went ashore to look in on a couple of bazaars, and buy a few small things and a pineapple to eat on board. The ship pressed on at a steady 350 miles per day. The weather was glorious, and I never tired of standing at the rail watching the sea, possibly thinking, possibly just staring. For two days we saw the fascinating and jagged blue coastline of Sumatra but thereafter we were in open sea. We glimpsed the occasional tanker or troopship bound for Singapore and Korea, soon to enter the seas that we had left behind - perhaps for ever.

The waters around us were always shining and silvery, reflecting the bright hot sun. They seemed to be alive and never still, always leaping about, frothing and foaming in rainbow crests around the ship's sides, and sometimes releasing exquisite little flying fish jumping from one wave to the next. It was never rough on this trip, but the heaving seas were always on the move as the fresh wind played over their surface. Through the Indian Ocean the troughs between the waves were often six feet deep, but the ship herself ploughed steadily onwards.

There was plenty to do on board. I was made responsible for a small troop-deck of Hussars from an armoured car regiment returning home after action in Malaya, and Knocker had made me promise to look after the returning National Service Dorset soldiers aboard. Bill Heald had been given the job of 'Training Officer', and as I knew him well, I was able to help him. Every morning at 6.45am we took PT for all ranks to try and keep ourselves fit. In addition I took over the job of running the ship's 'Range', as I had on the way out on the Fowey. As before, I stood on 'B' Deck in the very stern of the ship, checked no other ships were in the way, and threw crates over the back while four men armed with old rifles took pot shots at them as they bounced along the ship's wake until either they burst or disappeared in the distance. This I did daily during most of each morning and sometimes during the evening as well. It was very good for the soldiers, and as before very popular with all sorts of people - clerks, REME and Gunners who hadn't fired a rifle in years, the RAF, the Navy, the ship's crew, and even the ladies came along. It was a feature of the voyage - if a dangerous one - until it became unbearably hot in the Red Sea, but we resumed firing in the Med and even in the Atlantic until we entered the Bay of Biscay.

In the evenings, lots of entertainment was provided. While the weather was warm but not excessively hot we dressed each evening in thick Blues trousers, white shirt and black tie; there was a band on board that played in the main saloon; we were shown three films each week; and we had amusing evenings of housey-housey and horse-racing on the Promenade Deck.

Colombo was a delightful break. We docked early on a Monday and were able to spend all morning ashore. Once again I was fascinated by the city, and found it the pleasantest and most beautiful city we had visited in the East. I admired the fine 'colonial' buildings in the city centre; drove in our taxi along the grand water-front to the Officers' Swimming Club just beyond the Galle Face Hotel, very close to the sea. There we swam and drank coffee in a large crowd from the ship until well into the morning. After returning to the shops and buying a pair of elephant bookends, I went back to the boat in an open 1930 vintage Bentley, falling to bits, rattling like a lot of saucepans, complete with Claxton horn, and a jovial taxi driver. My final purchase was a handful of pineapples for a couple of bob.

As we sped homewards, the weather was exhilarating and the boat steady; so we were able to do three hours firing a day, between 9 and 12 noon in the stern at the "Range". In the afternoons I was free - but not bored. I spent some time on what the Army called "interior economy" and more on the top deck, shirtless in a deck chair. I read a novel a day, and did some solid reading to make up for the fact that I had read only a couple of books during my nine months in Hong Kong. Wind and sun converted me into a toast colour; I was almost black - the stage of being brown was over - unkind people nicknamed me 'wog'.

I thought Aden to be an ugly bare rock with a dirty town by the coast. I was awed by the mountains that towered over the Crater, full of crags, chasms, caves, burning light, deep shadow, and hazy mystery. Ashore the shops were disappointing, but there was much of interest in the goats and camels in the streets, the veiled Arab women, and the side alleys down which one glimpsed the traditional East - flat roofed stone Arab houses, foul bazaars, tough dusky men and naked children in narrow dusty streets.

We went to the civilian bathing beach several miles outside town, in a beautiful spot right under the mountains. We were relieved to find the swimming in the sea was wired off from the ocean to keep out the sharks, and were able to relax on a lovely coral beach with a good bar. I had hoped to contact the Duttons[2], who had lived in the Brooke House flat at one time, but could not make myself understood when I spoke to the telephone exchange. When we were hungry, we were driven to the Officers' Club in the town for a meal, but thought it poor, expensive, dilapidated and wholly lacking in attraction. We could not find a decent hotel and returned to the ship in the middle of the blazing afternoon.

After Aden it grew still hotter. For a while a gentle breeze cooled the air,

---

2 My parents had divided up Brooke House towards the end of the war and let part of it out to RAF officers and their families flying from Luton airport, and Alan Dutton and his wife had been one our first tenants. On demobilisation he joined the Colonial Service and served in South Arabia for many years.

but approaching the Suez Canal, we lay gasping on the deck chairs under the awnings, wiping away beads of perspiration with a towel. We had to cancel the training as it was too uncomfortable on the blistering deck, and gave up trying to fire on my 'Range' when the rifle metal became too hot to touch. Finally the first class passengers rebelled against having to dress for dinner, and organised a night-club called The Willow Inn after a notorious dive in Kowloon. We put awnings up on the Promenade Deck with coloured lights and gay flags. The troops provided a 'swing band' and we set aside a typical pocket-handkerchief dance floor. The dress was 'palm beach rig' which was interpreted very freely. It was often given a Chinese twist. I considered that a deck-chair canvas wound round my waist in the form of a sarong was most suitable.

Neguib, the Egyptian dictator, was held to be unreliable and his army to be trigger-happy, even though British troops were stationed along the Canal. We were therefore ordered to mount an armed guard and post sentries all round the ship while making the over-night passage of the Suez Canal. I was put in charge of the guard and had little sleep, but went round and round the darkened ship checking the alertness of the sentries as we quietly sailed up to the Bitter Lakes and onward in our convoy. When dawn came up we were still moving through the northern half of the Canal and watched curiously the life on both banks. Sometimes we passed British troops in armoured cars painted 'desert yellow'; at other times we sailed by long camel caravans; and once we were thrilled to see two Arabs in full fig riding great white camels.

At Port Said we were delayed twenty four hours with engine trouble. Meanwhile we were required to maintain our security precautions while lying at anchor in the harbour undergoing repair. I therefore lost another night's sleep as I spent most of the hours of darkness on the bridge of the ship with views all around and good communications with my sentries. It was not until 3am that I saw the crew 'close up' and the ship slowly creep forward into the outward channel, past the bright lights of the town and the mole, and out into the Mediterranean. The soldiers returned their arms and ammunition to the store, and the guard finally got some sleep.

For the following few days the ship hurried westwards and we re-opened The Willow Inn as an excuse for wearing the coolest possible clothing, drinking too much and entertaining ourselves through the warm evenings. They were filled with farewell cocktail parties, celebration dinners, the children's fancy dress and grown-up parties, but they were premature. The boilers still gave trouble, and to the huge irritation and concern of all the passengers we had to go into Malta for repairs.

Valletta

It was a beautiful day when we entered the fine harbour at Valletta. The waters were always bustling. All around us were launches, lots of boats looking like Venetian gondolas, barges, naval ships, ferry boats, and a floating dock, while little naked boys dived off the quay wall for pennies thrown into the water below them. The shore was crowded with sight-seers, and the roads along the harbour wall were busy with delivery vans, trucks, 'desert brown' military vehicles and even tourist pony-carts.

We spent five days sitting in the middle of the harbour and were able to use the ship as a hotel while the engineers laboured in heat of allegedly around 130 degrees to repair the engines. In a group of fellow officers, I went ashore each day and up the lift into the town, both to see the sights and to swim. We drank at the Phoenicia Hotel and called in all sorts of sleazy bars up and down the narrow streets. The swimming was always superb. Back on board late each afternoon, we change into long trousers before returning ashore for a meal and another drink or two in one of the little restaurants where we would stay listening to music and chatting until late at night.

On three mornings, I went out on my own to explore the little Maltese towns and take some exercise walking though the island countryside. On one very hot day when the temperature was said to be 99 degrees, I walked around the old walls of Rabat. Another day I visited the Cathedral and was greatly impressed with the tombs of the Knights of St John of Malta. On the third morning I went into the old town of Medina and wandered among the fine old houses in its narrow streets. A little old guide took me round the church where I found words inadequate to express my delight at its charm and beauty. That afternoon I went round the Valletta Palace and the Hall of St Michael and St George, and looked inside the cathedral to see the Caravaggio.

The soldiers on board were growing impatient with the delay, but we were placated by the loan of army landing craft to take parties of men and officers by sea to enjoy the swimming from deserted beaches. Early one morning, I accompanied a large number of troops on a big landing craft that took us round the island to St Thomas' Bay. There we were all able to swim on - as it were - our own private beach.

That evening, Dick Campbell and I and a couple of others decided to explore 'The Gut', the Valletta Red Light district of rough bars and brothels. After a poor meal and several beers, we went down a flight of steps and a filthy little alley into a dingy bar where we found ourselves talking to some drunken members of the Clyde crew. They jostled and baited us as we walked back to the harbour and insisted on accompanying us in the gondola that ferried us across to the ship. Boarding the troopship, I pushed them off vigorously. As a result, they singled me out for their unpleasant attentions. At the top of the gangway I was seized.

"Let go of me! You're drunk!"
"What did you say about the merchant navy?"
"Nothing. Let go!"

Two of the crew held my wrists and a third swung round and punched me hard with his fist on the right cheek. It was painful and humiliating. I was both frightened and angry. I pulled myself free and was about to hit back when Dick Campbell who was behind me rapidly intervened, pulled me away from the crewmen and hustled me down the companion way before I could think of retaliating. No doubt the crew were looking for a brawl and Dick was right to get me away. I was seething with rage but my fellow officers pushed me firmly into my cabin and told me to go to bed.

Next morning, I had a mild headache when a telegram was handed me from Liz who had just heard I was stuck on Malta, *"Suggest contact Wendy and Peter Glover[3], Colonel attached to RAF HQ. Love to them and you. Liz."*

I rang Peter in his office from the Phoenicia and was promptly invited over for tea, a bathe and dinner that night. A car met me at the top of the lift and I was whisked across to the Glovers' quarters at St Andrew's where I was treated as one of the family. All the children were home and we went off for a bathe in a pretty little cove followed by a huge tea, tennis, drinks, a family supper and

---

3 The Glovers had been great friends of my sister Liz when they had served together under Lord Mountbatten at the HQ of South East Asia Command (SEAC) in Singapore in 1945. Peter Glover retired as a Major General and Colonel Commandant of the Royal Artillery.

quiet conversation in their sitting room. It was a happy ending to our over-long enforced stay on Malta.

Homeward bound

The island was a fine sight as it lay on the port beam in the sunlight when we cruised slowly out into the Mediterranean, and turned westwards towards Gibraltar. To pass the time on the last leg of this long voyage, we resumed our former training programme, with PT on deck in the early morning, followed by firing on the 'range' at the ship's stern, where we organised team competitions. It rained and became much cooler, and for almost the first time since the previous April, I wore a shirt all day. The sea and the sky turned grey. We were going home.

We dug our old battledress uniforms out of our kit bags and dusted them down as we entered the Atlantic which was a good deal rougher than the Med. There was then another round of the usual end-of-voyage festivities; more noisy children's parties, a farewell dinner - which became a riot with streamers, balloons and paper hats - a grown-up fancy dress show, a dance, and a drinks party for subalterns in the Commandant's cabin. Our last day at sea was spent packing our trunks and cases with the Welsh coast on the starboard skyline. My baggage was two tin trunks, a green bedding roll, a suitcase and two parcels - one containing a bulky pair of book-ends, the other a pair of large circular Chinese hats.

We tied up to a pier in Liverpool docks very early on the morning of 10th August 1953. My parents had driven up from Luton, spent the night at the Adelphi Hotel, and came down to the docks after breakfast but there was a mix-up. They expected to be able to pick me up and take me back by car to Brooke House, but I had been instructed to escort the Dorset soldiers to the Depot in Dorchester. Early in the voyage I had written home to explain this commitment but my letter had been held up at the Army Post Office in Singapore where we subsequently learned a postal clerk had been prosecuted for hiding mail bags. I was horrified to see them and felt very guilty that I could only exchange a few words before I rushed to catch the train south with the men and their baggage. It was a fearful shame as my dear parents had driven up in the expectation of taking me home with them, but there was no help for it. We were able only to have a brief conversation before I tore off to the station. I was seriously embarrassed, but there was nothing I could do.

Worse was to come. The three of us subalterns clambered into a first class compartment, with the baggage stacked in a luggage van next door while the troops travelled farther down the train in the third class, and off we sped. Our carriage was held at Crewe for rather a long time and my fellow officers and I were horrified to see the soldiers' compartments slide past our window. To our shocked surprise we learned that their half of the train had been detached and was to terminate at Birmingham instead going on to Bristol and the south west. We were in a panic; we seemed to have dismally failed to fulfil our orders to escort the Dorset soldiers safely back to the Depot. We decided that my two colleagues should stay in the train to ensure the baggage reached Dorchester, and I should jump off when we pulled into Birmingham and search for the missing men. So I got off the train in a great stew, only to find the men relaxed and snoozing in a siding, unworried by their predicament. I hustled them on to another train going south, and was immensely relieved when, by a complicated route and with a couple of changes, we finally reached Dorchester not long after the others arrived with the baggage. All was well in the end, but the worry had taken a few years off my life.

I left the men in the bar of the King's Arms and walked up to the Depot. I found it completely unchanged. Everything was just as I had left it; many old friends were still there in the Officers' Mess and gave me a warm welcome. After a hectic day, the three of us home from the Far East enjoyed a pleasant, friendly and relaxing evening.

The following morning I talked to the new Depot Adjutant and learned two things. I had been promoted to full Lieutenant the previous March but nobody had bothered to let the Battalion know in Hong Kong. Secondly, the Battalion had not gone to Korea; they had packed everything up, had had a round of farewell parties, sent the colours and silver home out of harm's way, diverted a draft of 80 newly-trained men to join the Royal Hampshire Regiment, and then suffered a fearful anti-climax by being required to remain at San Wai - and there they stayed for another year before eventually moving to Korea.

The Colonel of the Regiment was in the Mess at lunchtime and was kind enough to drink my health. In a formal meeting with the Adjutant I handed over my identity cards and received my discharge from the Army. By 6pm I left the Depot a civilian once more. I was given a lift with my bags to the station and reached Brooke House in good order around 11pm that night. It was good to be home.

The 1st Dorsets' Detachment at the Coronation
Left to Right: Pte A Stanley, Pte D Sinnick, Sgt C Robertson, Lt R A F Reep, CSM J Underwoood, Lt D B Edwards, Sgt J Fellowes, Pte C Phillips, Cpl F Gough and Capt C A Morris

Chapter 5

Hong Kong 1953-54

*If you can fill the unforgiving minute
With sixty seconds' worth of distance run...*
         From *If* by Rudyard Kipling.

Shortly before Dick Eberlie left Hong Kong the 1st Dorsets sent a detachment which, together with a similar detachment from the 4th Battalion and a third from the Depot, represented the Dorset Regiment at the Coronation. The ten men from the 1st were commanded by Captain Tony Morris. Several members of the Battalion, including Knocker White, the Quartermaster, RSM Webber, Bandmaster John Plant, RQMS Vaughan, CSM James, Colour Sergeant Lloyd and Sergeant Robertson later received the Queen's Coronation Medal while CSM Mick Trodd was awarded the British Empire Medal in the Birthday Honours List.

That summer, ever conscious of regimental history, Knocker White marked the appointment of HRH The Duchess of Kent as Colonel-in-Chief of the Regiment with a Proclamation Parade. He wrote in the Regimental Journal that the appointment *completes the series of royal marks of favour which have been conferred on the Regiment since the first Royal Duke presented the officers of the 54th with the four hundred guinea punch bowl. Fifty years later the Duke of Kent's daughter, Her Majesty Queen Victoria, paid a visit to the 54th at Devonport and ordered that the officers should bear the Sphinx with Marabout above the numerals on their forage caps... During the same visit HRH The Prince Consort brought the*

Saluting the Punch Bowl: The Colonel-in-Chief's Proclamation Parade

young Prince of Wales and Prince Alfred to the Officers' Mess to view the punch bowl presented by their grandfather. As Dick Eberlie recalls in an earlier chapter, at the Colonel-in-Chief's Proclamation Parade the same punch bowl was placed on a table in front of the saluting base and the entire Battalion marched past at the salute.

Now, on Sunday 13th December 1953, a Ceremonial Parade was held to mark the Colonel-in-Chief's birthday. *For this parade we revived an old custom peculiar to the old 54th. Now that we are armed with our own 17-pounder anti-tank guns, one of which is named 'Marabout', we were able to fire a gun salute in honour of the occasion. …one of the last occasions that this salute was fired was at a General Inspection in Madras in 1839, at which time the point was most clearly made that the 54th, of all the Regiments of the Line, was alone entitled to make this particular form of salute. At any event, the effort was most satisfactory. We wonder what notes were made in the OP reports of the Chinese Communist Army across the border that morning.*

As the *Dorset Daily Echo* made clear for those in England, after a year the

Captain Tony Jelley escorting Senator Richard Nixon, November 1953

Dorsets had made themselves very much at home in the New Territories and had transformed San Wai Camp into *Little Dorchester*, which included a Bridport Road, a Cornhill and Poundbury Lines and Chickerell Lines.

The freshly-painted black and white signs now give the camp a very definite homely touch. The tiny concrete refuelling station, with its single pump, has been named the Grove Service Station. Greys Bridge spans the River Frome - a shallow stream which meanders through the centre of the camp and differs mainly from its Dorset counterpart in that an assault course, which crosses it, has caused many an anxious minute in the lives of troops trying to crawl over the single thread of bucking rope without getting uncomfortably wet in the stream below.

The camp's main road crosses the River Frome and climbs up, past Able, Baker and Charlie Company Lines, where it forms a roundabout and then retraces its steps back to the Guard Room. The roundabout has been named Top o'Town...

In November Support Company under Captain Tony Jelley found the Guard of Honour for the American Vice-President, Richard Nixon, who flew into Kai Tak Airport. With a more developed sense of history than tact, the Guard mounted with the Regimental Colour of the 2nd Battalion who, as the 54th Regiment of Foot, landed at Long Island in 1776. Senator Nixon congratulated the Band on their rendering of the *Star Spangled Banner*.

Back at home, the *Daily Echo* reported the Battalion's celebrations at Christmas, which for most of them must have been the warmest festive season in their lives. On 22nd December a Christmas tree party for their fifty-eight accompanying families was followed by an evening party in the Corporals' Mess, where Regimental Quartermaster Sergeant Jackie Vaughan ran a very successful game of *Housey Housey*. On Christmas Eve the massed bands of 27 Brigade (including the Dorsets' own band) beat retreat by searchlight on San Wai playing fields before a buffet supper in the NAAFI and carols. Christmas Day was celebrated traditionally by the warrant officers and sergeants waking the soldiers with tea in bed, and by their dinners being served by the officers and sergeants. On a very windy Boxing Day the officers played the sergeants at football, losing 3-1, while several inter-company six-a-side matches enabled others to join in the sport.

Knocker White at Christmas Party with Capt John Archer in front of blackboard

The year 1953 had been a good one for the Dorsets, whose excellence on the sports field had been mirrored by their military prowess. Support Company were jubilant. The Anti-Tank Platoon had won the Hong Kong Land Forces Anti-Tank Platoon competition while the Machine Gun Platoon had come equal first in their category. Their success must have been especially cheering for the members of the Anti-Tank because, earlier in the year, three of their old stagers - Privates Edgar Foot, Baldwin and *Darky* Barnes - had been seriously injured in an encounter with an express train.

On 11th January 1954, A Company provided the Guard for a visit by the newly appointed and newly knighted Commander-in-Chief of Far Eastern Land Forces (FARELF), Lieutenant-General Sir Charles Loewen. Five days later they were visited by the Deputy Chief of the Imperial General Staff. Lieutenant-General Sir Dudley Ward was originally a Dorset. After Wimborne Grammar School he served three years in the ranks before being commissioned into the Dorset Regiment in 1929, shortly before Knocker White. Ward did what for White would have been quite unthinkable: in 1937 he left the

Anti-Tank Platoon Accident

Dorsets to gain promotion in the King's Liverpool Regiment. Now Colonel of the King's, he was on his way to visit them. Such was this visitor's seniority that, tongue straying into cheek, Colonel White confessed that, for once, even he was *stumped for a regimental precedent for mounting a Guard of Honour on a member of the Army Council. We think we must remain stumped because in the comparatively short life of fifty years of the Army Council, as we know it today, we have never before produced a member of that august body.* Apart from Knocker White, Sir Dudley found only Captain Slick Smithers, the Quartermaster, who knew him of old.

In the Regimental Journal Knocker White described, for the benefit of fellow Dorsets elsewhere, the difficulties posed by the constraints of National Service and the Python scheme, which returned soldiers prematurely to the UK. It is the heartfelt cry of a regular officer struggling to maintain a professional battalion manned by a constantly changing flow of short-term National Servicemen.

We have been sent to the Far East on a definite mission. We are nearer to the enemy than ever we were when stationed amongst them in Austria. We find ourselves between two wars. The one to the North for the moment stilled, the other to the South very hot. The reader at home might well be encouraged to think that we have nothing to worry about. Reinforcements arrive from time to time and are immediately absorbed. Absorbed is an under-statement - gobbled up is a much better expression. They are literally grabbed and taken from the boat with their knees still lily white and poured into the Specialist Platoons. There is no opportunity to continue or even catch up on their training because the Battalion must soldier on. Over us all hangs the Damocles Sword of Release and Python.

Release in an army based on National Service must be accepted. However efficient the Mess Waiter, however satisfactory the Company Storeman, however expert the Machine Gunner or Mortarman, one must appreciate that he is 'doing his time'. If he is a good citizen and therefore a good soldier he does his duty well. The one factor that really encourages the Company Commander to carry on against overwhelming odds is the manner in which the good National Serviceman tackles whatever job is given him. What is really hitting the First Battalion the nastiest crack it has received in years is Python. Under this scheme with the sinister name, a number of our best and most useful soldiers are being lost to the Battalion. The individuals are, of course, happy in a temporary posting from an unattractive Nissen hut on the frontier of

Lieutenant Gerald Blight airborne

Communist China to the UK, but each departure is a blow to the military efficiency and corporate life of the Battalion.

...We are thirty full Corporals under establishment. This has recently increased because nine of these Corporals are now members of the Sergeants' Mess. These nine new Sergeants are doing their best - and are doing well. But what we want are the scores of soldiers - of regular Dorset soldiers not 'extra-regimentally employed'. We have been abroad for a year now - we have made a sound reputation for ourselves in Hong Kong, but we still lack the strong regular nucleus of NCOs and men to maintain this reputation and help us carry all before us in whatever operational tasks we will be required to fulfil in 1954.

The lull in the war in Korea referred to early in White's piece was evidence of some progress in negotiations between the United Nations and the Chinese, which in early August 1953 saw the Chinese release many British prisoners of war, including Glosters captured at the Imjin River in April 1951. The Dorsets Band had been sent to Korea, where they played the British soldiers out. The Regimental Journal recorded the event.

As each party arrived Mr Plant [the Bandmaster] *played the appropriate regimental march. Their great thrill was in spotting the Dorsets serving in the ranks of the Glosters, amongst who was Lieutenant Alan Blundell, and giving them 'The Maid of Glenconnel'.*

On their way home, the ex-prisoners arrived in Hong Kong *in two main parties, the first in Asturias carrying the privates and junior NCOs. We found a number of our old reservists in the ranks, like Mr Hobbs, the RSM of the Glosters. Some of these had already spent most of World War II in the bag. The officers and senior NCOs came through about three weeks later in the Empire Orwell.*

A note of some of the Battalion's entrances and exits during a single month - March 1954 - supports the Colonel's view. On the 6th three officers, one sergeant and seventy-two soldiers joined, together with one officer and forty men from the Royal Warwicks, who were attached for training. A week later sixty-seven men left on the *Empire Trooper*, thirty-eight of whom were destined for Malaya. Four days later a draft of three officers and sixty soldiers of the Royal Warwicks left for Korea.

Coote's Grenadiers at the Tattoo

After Exercise Pikestaff in January, February brought the Dorsets victory in the FARELF Inter-Unit Athletics. In their two years in the Colony the Dorsets won this competition both years and this time they won by a clear margin of forty-one points over their nearest rival, the 27th Heavy Anti-Aircraft Regiment, whose performance pushed the Royal Norfolks into third place. They also won the Brigade Athletics at Kowloon while the Dorsets also beat the Royal Norfolks 8-3 at boxing. A new arrival was Captain *J B* Smith, who had spent the last two years in Burma. After a spell as Intelligence Officer, *J B* (as he was known in the Regiment) would succeed John Archer as Adjutant.

March saw a second visit by Lieutenant-General Sir Charles Loewen. Accompanied by the GOC and the Brigade Commander, he watched company training. Having been a mountain gunner, he was especially interested in the Battalion's anti-tank guns and their supporting mule section.

At the beginning of the month Knocker White had confirmed his plan that the Dorsets' farewell to Hong Kong should be a tattoo, which would echo the one he had masterminded two years before in Dorchester and those his father had organised in the 1920s. Conceived on a characteristically grand scale, this 1954 Tattoo would celebrate the bi-centenary of the 39th Regiment's arrival in India - *Primus in Indis* - and its theme would be India. Four important incidents of regimental history would be re-enacted: the 39th at the Battle of Plassey in 1757, the 54th aboard the *Sarah Sands* on their way to the Indian Mutiny in 1857, the 1st Battalion in the Tirah in 1897 and the 2nd Battalion's triumph at Kohima in 1944. The task of re-enacting Plassey fell to Captain Geoff Stewart's A Company, the *Sarah Sands* to Captain Steve Elvery's D Company, the Tirah to Captain Tony Morris's C Company (supported by the Dorset Mule Section of 81 Pack Troop, RASC) and Kohima to B Company under the newly arrived Major *Henry* Hall (supported by the 7th Royal Tank Regiment).

A decorated veteran of Arnhem, *Henry* Hall - nicknamed after the bandleader - must have approached with some trepidation the task of reconstructing the battle under the omnipresent nose of his new CO, who was one of its victors. Corporal Horace Dibben remembers helping to build the simulated water towers around the tennis court at Kohima. They had built them to stand tall until Knocker White appeared and told them to cut them down to ground level because the towers at Kohima had been much lower.

The Tattoo

In the Regimental Journal Knocker White remembered: *The setting was excellent. Once we had dragged the searchlights up to the top of the surrounding hills we had one of the most attractive amphitheatres a producer could wish for.* Preparations were hard and exacting work. He recalled *a lot of trouble with our Bren guns, which seemed to resent being fiddled around with to fire at the same speed as a Japanese Taisho. Also there was the question of ground. The whole key to the Kohima battle was the necessity to drive the Jap off his terraces. Terraces are very difficult to reproduce in a stadium. However, Major Hall and CSM James overcame all their many problems, and Kohima, because it was modern and therefore understood by every spectator more easily…, became one of the highlights of the evening.*

As at the original battle the tank stole the thunder. *We didn't try to disguise the Comet tank lent by our friends of A Squadron, 7th Royal Tanks - we just said that it represented a Lee-Grant. Its effect was terrific and it shook our guests to no mean extent as it blasted its way from bunker to bunker whilst Captain Chettle and Sergeant Given once again re-enacted their stirring deeds of 13th May ten years ago.*

Two outstanding athletes: L/Cpl Crane and Cpl Boddy

B Company's scenic effects, constructed by themselves, were most effective, especially the portable water tank which was carried on to the arena in the black out.

In C Company's recreation of the Tirah action Second Lieutenant Jimmy Hosking played Lieutenant Cowie (the first man on top of the hill at Dargai) and Corporal Miller re-enacted Private Vickery winning his Victoria Cross.

It was a spectacular and noisy entertainment. The Band and Drums, under John Plant and Drum Major Tommy Thomas, had to play long and work hard to compete with the perpetual small arms fire punctuated by the explosion as the stern of the *Sarah Sands* caved in and the head-splitting blast as the tank at Kohima fired its big gun. In the Kohima re-enactment, Horace Dibben played a Japanese soldier and, when the tank fired its blank shells, the crashes rang so loud that he and his comrades disgraced the Imperial Japanese Army by running like rabbits.

April saw the arrival of a new Second-in-Command, Major Rupert Wheatley, who joined the Battalion fresh from the Staff College, and of a new draft of two officers and seventy-six men. The Band and Drums and the Carrier Platoon,

ORQMS Ted Ralph MBE

under Tony Jelley, represented the Battalion at the Queen's Birthday Parade in Kowloon. One of the Battalion's star sportsmen, Lance-Corporal Crane of Headquarter Company, was doubly honoured, receiving the Hawkins Cup for the best individual athletic performance in 1953 and the Commanding Officer's Award for outstanding performance 1951-54. On the 27th a draft of four officers and sixty-seven soldiers joined the Battalion.

During their twenty-two months in Hong Kong the Dorsets lost three men, all in the Battalion's last six months in the Colony. The first, eighteen-year-old Private M Lawless, died of polio in the 33rd British Hospital on 24th February 1954, having served with the Battalion for only a few weeks. On 8th May Private Robert Henry Munday was drowned and on 30th June Private Edwin George Beales died of heat exhaustion. Tragedy also struck Colour Sergeant Nick Carter, who was flown home to England, where his wife was seriously ill. Sadly, Mrs Carter did not survive her illness.

The tenth anniversary of the Battle of Kohima, an event especially close to Knocker White's heart, was marked on 13th May. Another echo of Kohima was heard when the Royal Hong Kong Defence Force marked its centenary. The officer receiving the Queen's Colour on this occasion was Captain John O'Driscoll, who was commissioned into the Dorset Regiment in 1941 and led the 2nd Battalion's Guerrilla Platoon at Kohima with great enterprise and gallantry.

In June the Battalion paraded for group photographs to be taken for a Regimental album being compiled to commemorate the Battalion's time in Hong Kong, which was coming to an end. July began with a Brigade Commander's inspection. On the 8th Lance-Corporal Tourtel won the Commanding Officer's Bugle Competition and on the 9th the Dorsets' Motor Transport Section won the Brigade MT Competition.

Captain Tony Morris, one of the last remaining officers who had arrived in Hong Kong with the Battalion, now left to join HQ, British Forces, Hong Kong. Another departure was Orderly Room Quartermaster Sergeant Ted Ralph, who in July completed twenty-eight years' service. On ORQMS Ralph's last day with the Regiment he was presented with the MBE by Lieutenant-General Sir Cecil Sugden. On 16th July the Battalion was joined by Sergeant Norman Elgie, who had won the Military Medal with the 1st Battalion in North West Europe.

On the 18th the Bishop of Hong Kong preached at the Battalion's farewell service, attended by more than 500 Dorsets and held in the large dining hall in the Marabout Lines of San Wai Camp. It was a time of arrivals and departures. National Servicemen with most time to serve continued with the Battalion to Korea while those with less time joined the Royal Hampshires in Malaya. A few, ineligible for Korea perhaps because they were not yet nineteen, were sent to join the Welch Regiment. The Dorsets' Advance Party arrived in Korea just in time to qualify for the United Nations Korea Medal. Thus it was that only those in the Band (who had visited Korea in 1953) and the Advance Party would qualify for the campaign medal.

On 4th August 1954 the main party of the 1st Dorsets left San Wai Camp. Knocker White wrote in the Regimental Journal: *It is with little regret that we leave the New Territories. We have already handed over our 'Hadrian's Wall' and all its irritating commitments. Our advance party is already in Korea and, despite their already having encountered the worst of the Korean wet weather, they are from all accounts in great form and fully subscribe to the optimistic opinion of their new station formed by the Commanding Officer on his reconnaissance in June…*

Band playing on Battalion leaving Hong Kong

As long as the oldest serving soldier can remember, rain is a necessary accompaniment to any move of a Dorset battalion. Here in Hong Kong, where the summer rains have been abnormally light and a deal of anxiety is caused by the low level of the reservoirs, it only took the move of the Battalion from San Wai Camp for a typhoon lurking in the Pacific to direct its course on the China coast.

However, reports from the advance party, settling down near the south bank of the River Imjin thirty miles north of Seoul, the capital of the Republic of Korea, indicate that our present treatment can be classed as mere April showers compared with what they are getting on the 38th Parallel.

A week later, with their Band playing, the Battalion sailed aboard HMT *Devonshire* for new adventures with the United Nations forces in Korea. As they embarked on that wet, windy day in August 1954, none could know that Korea was to be the 1st Battalion's penultimate overseas posting and that, within four years, the Dorset Regiment would amalgamate with their friends and neighbours the Devons.

The Queen's Birthday Parade, Kowloon 1953

1ˢᵗ Dorsets ready to leave for Korea

The Officers

Back Row: Second Lieutenants J C Rogers, D R Gibson, D J Wakeley, P M Merrikin, C G C Hosking, A N Solomons, J W Hambly, S M Alley, G Pitman

Third Row: Lieutenants J D F Jenks, E C Campbell, B G L Hebden, J B St V Hawkins, Second Lieutenant R A de L H Bembridge, Lieutenants A R Tawney, P N Elgar, D W Taylor, Second Lieutenant A P Jones

Second Row: Captains J Meeres, M J Reynolds, Lieutenant R A F Reep, Second Lieutenant J W Tong, Captains R H B Feltham, E C Stones, H L K Jones, Lieutenant D B Edwards, Second Lieutenant J Ives, Captains H C Ealand, C E K Speller, A J Smoker

Front Row: Captains A G Jelley, J B Smith, C A Morris, J Drew, Majors A A P C Thomas TD, R H Wheatley DSO, Lieutenant-Colonel O G W White DSO, Captain and Adjutant A J Archer, Majors M Williams, R F Hall MC, Captains G M Stewart, J F Wreford, Captain and Quartermaster L T Smithers.

Inset: Captain S S Elvery

On Cloudy Hill 3,600 feet up and overlooking the Chinese border
At front left to right: John Curl, Pte Way, Cocoa Brain, L/Cpl Trowbridge
Standing at rear: Bob Little and Pte Graham

B Company led by Lt John Ives and CSM Jimmy James MM

The Sergeants and Warrant Officers with guests from HMS Cossack
Fourth Row: Sergeants H Harrison (RAPC), P Chant, R Boon, W Floyd,
L Lingard, B Scott, J Crummack, J Cleverley, A Brehaut, S Coles,
J Freeman (APTC), G Moss, E Robinson (Royal Warwicks), C Mitchell, J Jephcote
Third Row: Sergeants H Outerside, A Bongard, R Miles, W Wood (REME),
W Lucas, R Brooks, F Creech, Drum Major R Thomas, Sergeants, J Ellis,
E Clifton, H Freeth, J Maxted, C Roberston, G Hayward, C Smith
Second Row: Colour Sergeants L Cleeve, A Tizzard,
Company Sergeant-Majors H French, R F James MM, J Russell, V Howe,
RQMS W H Vaughan, RSM L Webber, ORQMS W A G Ralph MBE,
Company Sergeant-Majors L Pitman, K Marquis, S Wells,
Colour Sergeant G F Trodd BEM, F Glanville, P Blissett
Front Row: Guests from HMS Cossack

The Corps of Drums
Rear: N Langman, McGee, J Lumber, R Coleman, C Bannion, D Harvey, H Ford
Middle: N Clarke, Langman, D Cole, Withstone, B Rendell
Front: L/Cpl F Tourtel, G Easment, L/Cpl K Shiner, Cpl R Hannaford, Drum Major G Thomas, Cpl G Young, L/Cpl R Harmer and Drummers Thorne and Jordan

1st Dorsets Athletics Team - Winners of HKLF Championship 1953
Back Row: 2/Lt Eberlie, Pte Reed, Pte Borley, L/Cpl Scott, Bdsm Moiser, Pte Capstick, 2/Lt Marx, Pte Phillips, L/Cpl Brown, Cpl Knight, L/Cpl Parker, Fus Davey.
Middle Row: Pte Hunt, Cpl Freeth, Cpl Boddy, 2/Lt Edwards, Lt Reep (Captain), Lt-Col White, Lt Blight, Sgt Tizzard, L/Cpl Crane, Sgt Pearce, Sgt Smith.
Front Row: Fus Samain, Pte Lock, Pte Gordon, L/Cpl Atkins, Pte Trigger, Pte Hobby, Pte Chapp, Fus Roussay

Commanding
1ST BN THE DORSET REGIMENT
(Thirty Ninth & Fifty Fourth)

12 FEB 54.

THE FORMATION OF THE REGIMENT

Two hundred and fifty two years ago on 13 FEB 1702, King WILLIAM III, just before his sudden death, signed the Royal Warrant authorising Colonel Richard Coote to raise a regiment of foot in IRELAND on the new higher establishment of twelve Companies each of three Officers, three Sergeants, two Drummers and Fifty Privates.

In 1742 the Regiment was granted the number XXXIX and sixty five years later it became associated with the county of DORSET through the award of the title "39th or DORSETSHIRE REGIMENT of FOOT".

In 1881 the British Infantry was re-organised into County Regimental Groups of Regular, Militia and Volunteer Battalions. As a result the DORSET REGIMENT as we know it today was formed as follows

    1st Battalion from the 39th (DORSETSHIRE) Regiment
    2nd Battalion from the 54th (WEST NORFOLK) Regiment
    3rd Battalion from the DORSET MILITIA
    1st Volunteer Battalion from the DORSET RIFLE VOLUNTEERS

The 54th had been raised in 1755 by Colonel John CAMPBELL. Traditionally the Regimental March, The Maid of Glenconnel dates from the earliest days of the 54th.

The DORSET MILITIA were by far the oldest "UNIT" in the new County Group. They were the descendants of the old Saxon Fyrd and could trace their existence as an organised body to as far back as 1660. At the battle of SEDGEMOOR, they were known as the "Red Regiment of DORSET MILITIA". From about 1757 until 1881 they bore the figure 'I' on their accoutrements to indicate their seniority in the English Militia.

The DORSET RIFLE VOLUNTEERS had been raised at BRIDPORT in 1859 (Volunteer Infantry Units had been raised in the County during the French Wars of half a century earlier). They have now an unbroken record of service of nearly one hundred years.

In 1908 the 1st Volunteer Battalion became the 4th(TF) Battalion and in 1922 the 4th(TA) Battalion.

In 1922 the 3rd Battalion was placed in suspended animation, and was finally disbanded in 1953.

In 1949 the 1st and 2nd Battalions were formally amalgamated with the title 1st Battalion The DORSETSHIRE Regiment at a parade held in MEIDLING BARRACKS, VIENNA.

In 1951 HM King GEORGE VI approved of the title of the Regiment being altered to THE DORSET REGIMENT.

...................../2

One of Knocker White's historical Orders of the Day

B Company on exercise
Centre at rear: Lt John Ives, Major Henry Hall MC
Front from left: CSM Jimmy James MM, Lt Gerald Blight, Sgt Tommy Thomas
and two unknown soldiers

Colonel's Staff Car with Pte Bill Osmond

Six men ready for guard duty

*S Company march on to Remembrance Day Parade 1953 led by
Maj Morris Williams and CSM Ken Marquis*

Medium Machine Gun Platoon
Back Row: G Sargeant, J Hooper, R Little, A Trout, C Rolls, J Rich, J Lampin, B Hewitt, W Langtree, C Brain, ?, G Chase, C Westerside (REME)
Middle Row: L/Cpl Robinson, R Blake, Regan, Burnett, Curtis, Draper, C Coward, Rice, R Baker, J Curl, E Savage, W Eden, Sheppard
Front Row: Graham, Cannon, L/Cpl Downton, L/Cpl Trowbridge, Cpl Ellis, Sgt Gibb, Lt-Col O G W White DSO, Maj I Ramsay, Sgt P Chant, Cpl W Woodley, Cpl Foote, L/Cpl J Stockley, H Bulford
Machine-gunners: Edney (left) and Way (right)

Christmas Party 1953

Lunchbreak in the heat

Bandmaster John Plant conducts the Band and Drums

Colonel-in-Chief's Birthday Parade

17-pounder Anti-tank Guns

Six Dorsets enjoying Hong Kong
Left to right: John Curl, Paddy Whiffen, F Challacombe, R Judd, Bert Sandford and Ken Rowland

Parade at Kowloon

Chapter 6

Memories

🍎 🍎 🍎

Though much is taken, much abides...
From *Ulysses* by Alfred, Lord Tennyson

🍎 🍎 🍎

The Dorset Regiment Old Comrades who meet at the Keep Museum for coffee on the last Wednesday of each month are mostly ex-National Servicemen from the 1950s. Among them are several veterans of Hong Kong who share many of Dick Eberlie's memories. This final chapter includes some of their recollections together with those of a few others who served with the 1st Dorsets at that time.

Privates Tony Marsh and Dave Chant joined the Regiment at the Depot on 4th December 1952. The officer in command of training their batch of recruits was Major Ivor Ramsay, who soon afterwards departed for Hong Kong. After their six weeks' basic training Ramsay's successor, Captain Darts Dartnall, told their squad that, instead of going on to Exeter for their continuation training, they would be going straight to the Battalion. On HMT *Asturias* they arrived in Hong Kong in early 1953 and were both posted to Support Company, who occupied Poundbury Lines and were now commanded by Ivor Ramsay. Tony joined the Machine-gun Platoon under John Wreford (who had fought with the 5th Dorsets at Arnhem) and later under Tony Jelley, while Dave spent a couple of months in the Mortar Platoon before transferring to the Corps of Drums.

They were struck by the extreme poverty of some of the local population, who lived in shanties protected from the elements by sheets of battered

Privates Pat Norris, Harry Chandler, Tony Marsh and John Bryant of S Company loose in Hong Kong

Drummer David Chant

linoleum. Many shared their pitiful accommodation with pigs and chickens while their children begged for ten cents. Others occupied ancient boats in the harbour. From the Dorsets' observation posts on the hill north of the camp, they could see across the border into China, where they were horrified to see public hangings taking place.

Their vivid memories include border patrols, exercises crossing flooded paddy fields where they somehow accumulated leeches inside their jungle boots, a fire in the shanty town on the hillside which rendered tens of thousands homeless, the devastation caused by Typhoon Susan, and guard duty on the gate of San Wai Camp which lasted twenty-four hours - in blocks of two hours on and four off.

From Hong Kong Tony and Dave were sent together to join the 1st Royal Hampshires in Malaya, where they were posted to different companies. Tony's company commander was none other than Ivor Ramsay, in whose steps he had trodden from Dorchester to Hong Kong and finally to Malaya.

Private Frank Read remembers how, on his voyage out, at Port Said the ship was soon *surrounded by small craft selling every souvenir you could think of, ropes were set up between the ship's deck and the small craft, and the bartering then began. It consisted of the buyer shouting out to the seller "You send the goods up." Then the seller would say "No." …after a bit of argy bargy one of them would give in - generally the buyer - and send his money down to where the grateful seller would shout out "Thank you, John", and proceeded to paddle off with the money. …a couple of the ship's crew… said "Leave them to us. We'll sort them out." Whereupon they rolled out the ship's sea water hoses and directed the full force of water at the vendors' boats. It took only a few minutes before the boats started turning upside down, all their souvenirs floating on top of the water and the vendors swimming around trying to retrieve as many goods as they could, shouting "Inglesi bastards!"*

On the last leg of their voyage across the South China Sea he remembered seeing floating in the sea *debris from properties that had been wrecked and palm trees that had been uprooted by the typhoon that had hit the Philippine Islands a couple of days earlier.*

He recalled that: *when we arrived at Kowloon Railway Station, we were met by that wonderful body of people, The Salvation Army, who gave us cups of tea and a bite to eat before we moved off…*

Local enterprise

On arrival at Fan Ling railway station we were met with about a dozen or so 3-tonners who took us and all of our kit to our new home at San Wai Camp. On arrival you can guess what happened: we were told "Drop your kit in your designated hut and then parade outside in full battle dress, because you ain't stopping. So move. Get your arses in gear. We're going up that bloody great hill over there to relieve the Middlesex Regiment and to take over their positions." There is nearly always a light at the end of the tunnel… We happened to have a Major in charge of us who was leading us up to our new positions overlooking Communist China. After we had got our positions marked out and got settled in the Major came round and asked us all did we want any cigarettes. The majority of us said "Please!" In a short time a ration truck arrived with our cigarettes; each of us had a packet of twenty. I cannot remember who the Major was, but he was definitely our hero that day.

Lance-Corporal Jeff Eckersall remembers the dilapidated state of San Wai Camp on their arrival and the work involved to clean it up and cut the grass. His memory is of very hot weather, terrible smells and the RSM's Parade on three Saturdays each month with the CO's drill parade on the fourth. As a newly promoted lance-corporal Jeff attended the twenty-first birthday party of a friend which was held in the Privates' Mess. RSM Webber gave him a severe telling off and removed all his privileges for three months.

Private Peter Lane was in the same intake as Jeff and recalls - with two others on jankers - cleaning the brass pieces of the fire pump. A Chinese boy arrived selling ice creams and the three bought one each. At that moment Sgt Gracie Fields arrived and the three defaulters thrust the ice creams into their pockets. Having inspected the pump and had a look around, Sgt Fields left, saying only: *And if you want to eat ice creams, keep them out of the way.*

He also remembers upsetting a dinghy while swimming in Repulse Bay and hoping there weren't any sharks about… A signaller, he was fitting telephone wire across the roof of one of the huts when he dislodged the remains of a broken chimney and a four or five foot length of it crashed through the roof and onto a table in the hut below, narrowly missing a soldier who had been sitting at the table reading the paper.

Private John Curl *arrived at San Wai Camp on December 15th 1952 (ten days before Christmas). The average age of most of the draft was eighteen. Homesick, tired and first impressions of San Wai did little to boost morale, especially when shown our billet of a Nissen hut with the majority of windows missing, overhead fans inoperative, therefore, bloody cold one minute with cold winds and stifling hot the next. We learnt later that the billet was a previous home for the Dorsets' regimental mules, which were obviously moved out in a hurry to accommodate us. By all accounts, San Wai was used during World War 2 by the Japanese as a prison camp*

After about three weeks, we were more than relieved to be assigned to various companies and the majority of our draft joined Support Company under Major Ramsay. Five Exmouth lads, including myself, joined Support Company. I was in the Machine Gun Platoon under the command of Capt. Wreford, followed later by Captain Jelley. John England joined the Mortar Platoon, 'Dilly' Edmonds and 'Titch' Frost joined the Assault Pioneer Platoon and Stan Maers became Major Ramsay's batman.

Support Company and D Company were not part of the main Battalion Camp and the river separating the two camps often flooded during the monsoon season. This sometimes made life quite pleasant with HQ not having complete control over Support and D Company, which of course tended to upset the CO and in particular the RSM.

Support Company, when the Dorsets took over, looked reminiscent of a bomb site but gradually the gardens were planted with flowers and somehow roses were obtained from some source and things did improve. The Nissen huts inside and out were painted. I do recollect, though, that on one occasion on a battalion exercise, at an RV 'Brew Up', Captain Jelley referred to San Wai Camp as one of the worst camps he had ever encountered. This was something of an unusual admission for an officer to make at the time.

Later, Major [Morris] Williams took over command of Support Company with Company Sergeant-Major [Ken] Marquis. Full credit to both, who under their leadership improved things immensely within the Company and always showed an understanding and sense of fair play… I found this particularly so when I was Company Clerk and saw the number of charges dropped on the OC's orders.

In spite of all, one can only reflect on the good times and the silly and stupid situations that occurred whilst stationed at San Wai. The CO, Lieutenant-Colonel O G White or 'Knocker' as he was affectionately known, was a stickler for intense training for the 1st Dorsets in preparation for Korea. Every Tuesday morning during the cooler months of the year, at 0600hrs and before breakfast (just a cup of tea), the whole battalion had to march to Shau Tau Kok, a border post overlooking Communist China - a total distance of nine miles. On one such march and to the delight of the troops, the RSM could not stand the pace and had to be driven back to San Wai on the back of the Provo Sergeant Gracie Fields's motorbike. We all thought this was hardly a good example to the troops regarding general fitness if the RSM wasn't up to standard.

I always looked forward to the five mile cross-country run every Wednesday (like hell) when Knocker would stand on the back of his Austin Champ dressed in normal military attire, with the exception being his hat (which was a Swiss alpine type hat with a protruding feather sticking out the top) and with the customary officers' stick in his hand. He would shout at the very reluctant participants with various comments, such as "That man - Get your Bloody Hair Cut". He shouted to me on one occasion when crossing knee-deep in a paddy field. I was more concerned about half my torso being completely covered in leeches and guarding my own private operational tackle than getting a 'bloody haircut'.

Then there was the platoon comedian - every platoon had one somewhere who kept morale up and Jim Hooper from Hamworthy could at times be that one. I remember the platoon was engaged in digging a series of Vickers Machine Gun bunkers 3,600ft above sea level on Cloudy Hill overlooking Communist China. The bunkers were about eight feet deep and about eight feet square, with a ladder to get in and out during construction, and we worked in teams with a break after about an hour because of the heat. Captain Jelley called our team, including Jim and myself, to get out for a much earned break and a brew. He praised our team for our hours of work. Jim Hooper, in an all very sincere voice explained to the Captain that he was writing a book about his National Service days, and that he had two titles in mind but could not make up his mind which one to use. Could Captain Jelley advise him on which title he should choose? The mood was more serious and so was the Captain, who agreed that he would be more than happy to help out.

"What titles have you come up with, Private Hooper?"

"Well, Sir, after today I can't decide whether to title the book 'Two Years in the Slave Trade' or 'Two Years of Human Bondage'."

Captain Jelley took it well and you can imagine the platoon in complete hysterics.

Private Gordon Pratten remembers disembarking at Kowloon, after five weeks aboard *Empire Fowey*, to see *the ladies had brightly coloured clothing with skirts split to high thigh. Military transport then took us through New Territories to Fan Ling close to the Chinese Border.*

I spent two weeks in Dog Company with fitness training up and down the nearby mountain of Tai Mo Shan. I then transferred into Support Company and the Mortar Platoon. This was much more acceptable - riding in Bren gun carriers and learning about transporting heavy gear onto mules, which were handled by Gurkha soldiers.

When off duty riding by train from Fan Ling into Kowloon and Hong Kong, we observed much poverty and tar-paper shacks, Nathan Rd, and the Peninsula Hotel, from which a group of us were asked to leave because of noisy behaviour.

Most of our duties consisted of patrolling the border with China and sorting out the troublesome villagers with illegal immigrants. Some of us were chosen as escorts at funerals of Service personnel who were buried in Happy Valley. Being part of a night-time Tattoo for the Governor of Hong Kong was a once in a life time experience, where we were told that our performance was as good as any he had seen.

Private Geoff Eavis recalls, immediately on arriving at San Wai Camp and meeting Sergeant Gracie Fields, being ordered to change into shorts and vest and to run to the top of Badge Hill. He remarks pointedly: *Anyone that has been there will know how hard that is after being at sea for six weeks.*

Sheppy's Carrier - Pte Roy Sheppard

Joining S Company, Geoff trained under Corporals *Oxo* Upton and Vic Farminer. *Our first manoeuvre was a live firing range at the rear of the camp. We had to go between the tapes to keep out of the minefields where the Assault Pioneers were waiting to blow us up. I was driving the lead carrier with the Medium Machine Gun Platoon Commander, Captain Jelley. I went the wrong side of the tape - all the others followed. Lance-Corporal Happy Harman blew us up. Till this day he has never forgotten this.*

I will never forget doing border guard at Shau Tau Kok and watching tens of thousands of Chinese soldiers doing PT a few hundred yards away. What ten of us would have done if they had attacked, I don't know.

Geoff remembers **Sergeant Vic Farminer**, *who joined the Dorsets in Austria from the Royal Hampshires. He was demobbed in 1952 but could not settle in civvy life so rejoined the Regiment in Hong Kong as Bren Gun Carrier Corporal. His first job was to train ten of us young 18-year-olds to drive carriers. One of the first things we did after we passed our test was to attend the Queen's Birthday Parade in Kowloon. Vic allowed us forty gallons of petrol and one gallon of oil to wash our*

Bunker on Cloudy Mountain

carriers and they looked fantastic. We went in convoy but, before we got to Fan Ling, which was about two miles, the dust had settled on the petrol and oil. Before we got to Kowloon they were in a worse state than before we cleaned them. So we parked up and had to clean them all over again. After the parade Vic said "I'm going to take you on the town tonight." We went to the Nine Dragons Club in Nathan Road, Kowloon, then over to the Cheerio Club in Hong Kong. I think every place he took us was out of bounds!

I remember Vic singing in the NAAFI on Saturday nights with Tony Marsh on the piano. We sang the old Support Company songs with piles of San Miguel bottles on the tables.

Corporal Michael Barton recalls *our primary object in the event of hostilities was to man the defence on Cloudy Mountain. …a constant guard was maintained on the lower approaches at Birds Hill Ammunition Point. On the reverse slope was a single concrete road for which, during exercises, a traffic control was kept. Accidents were rare but I was present when a truck toppled over the side sounding like a load of rusty cans as it galloped down the rocky abyss.* At the guard post, the *conditions,* *considering its function, were poor to say the least. The cooking was done by one of the local Chinese in a ramshackle hut. The sleeping facilities were just as bad, a tent for the guard commander and 2-i-C with the men in another - lighting at night by hurricane lamp. The tents must have been at that location for years. The ammunition was housed better than the men, in brick-walled huts. ...being half-way up a mountain, the amusements/entertainments were non-existent. All the water had to be brought in so keeping clean was difficult. At the end of the fifth day the return to camp and a refreshing shower was paramount in everyone's thoughts.*

It was April 1953 when the Regiment had to do the annual rifle and Bren qualifications and as a result my classification was first in both categories and I was Charlie Company leader. This entitled me to the sharpshooter's badge and additional pay. It also meant my inclusion in the Dorsets' team training at the naval ranges on Stonecutter's Island for several weeks with possible selection to represent the Battalion to shoot for the Governor's Twenty Competition at Kai Tak ranges. There were two ranges at Kai Tak parallel to each other. Sometimes the wind played tricks and the red flags, that were not only a warning but also an indication of wind strength, could be flying in contradiction to one another due to the topography. Planes landing at the nearby airport would fly low overhead with undercarriage down - quite disconcerting. The team did reasonably well even though competing against individuals with Vernier sights on their rifles. I believe Corporal Ennis and a few others managed to make the Governor's Twenty.

Lieutenant Gos Home was a guest of the Dorsets while training to join the Royal Fusiliers in battle in Korea. He remembers arriving with two other Fusilier subalterns, Claude Ash and Colin Shortis *fresh from Eaton Hall Officer Cadet School and a spell at The Tower of London. From a Duke's palace in Cheshire, to a Royal palace in London they could have felt that an army camp on the edge of China was a come down but no, they loved the Willow Pattern perfection of the Chinese countryside and the warm welcome they received from their military country cousins.*

Acclimatisation to the heat of the tropics, to the rigours of eastern hillsides and the skills of patrolling at night were well and truly on the agenda, but the setting was so beautiful - what with Fan Ling Golf Course, the local farming community which seemed more middle ages than 20th century, the charming bays for swimming (particularly Tai Po) and the views of mainland China (the very nation we were off to fight against) added to the mix of contrasts. I never succeeded in leading a patrol into any of the villages without a posse of dogs barking their heads off.

Colin Shortis and I shared a Nissen Hut where I would recover from all the injections that the Dorsets MO jabbed into my arms to prepare me for the assault of Korean 'mossies'. We had a very active weekend social life in Hong Kong and Kowloon and I have a photo of myself with a Dorset officer friend of mine taking tea in our white uniforms at the home of Hong Kong's Governor General, Sir Alexander Grantham. Colin, who was a real adventurer, somehow got himself all the way to Macau which was quite an achievement. Major Freer-Smith was my charming Company Commander, none nicer. We were also introduced to Dorset Dinner nights, which were quite rumbustious as I recall. One remaining memory was being trained in the handling of mules. We were all standing one morning learning about the oddities of this noble beast when a rather rotund Dorsets Sergeant, who was sitting crossed legged on the ground, suddenly rose like a helicopter screaming wildly as a snake fell out of his army shorts!

Gos Home's friend and fellow Royal Fusilier, **Lieutenant Colin Shortis**, later became a Dorset (and a Major-General). Looking back on his time in Hong Kong, Colin concludes that: *The more I thought about it the more I realised that what was so special about the Dorsets at that period was the extremely strong personality of the CO which pervaded the whole battalion and which inculcated a very strong Regimental spirit, the tremendous mess life with some very varied characters and the wonderful singing after Dinner with a mixture of West Country, Austrian folk and Nazi marching songs spiced up by Waltzing Matilda and Ten Men Went To Mow, both sung in Malay and you can guess where that came from!*

Geoffrey White was a most unusual man with an extremely strong personality and with total confidence in his own judgement. There were no half measures with him and if he felt that someone was not pulling his weight then he would remove him by sending him on report to other battalions within the Wessex Brigade where usually, but not always, the man did well. But what is certain is that, if the 1ˢᵗ Dorsets had been deployed on operations, they would have done very well under his command.

The other characteristic of the Battalion which struck an outside observer very forcibly was the close and happy relationship between all ranks, whether regular or National Service, officer or soldier. The vast majority came from the same West Country background, often they were the sons or nephews of the Regiment and there was a very genuine family atmosphere. The Dorsets had always done the business but always in a very understated way, as their history shows. I felt totally at home.

Their Colonel's obsessive fondness for the colour green resulted in Private Hobby having to repaint the regimental bus, which became known as the Green Linnet. **Lieutenant Bob Reep** remembers that: *Everything that could reasonably be painted, including (technically incorrect) our vehicles' Tac signs, assumed that colour. Occasionally this colour was perhaps overdone. For example, after a heavy defeat by 1 WELCH at rugby, some of our men crept one night into the Welch camp, situated a short distance across the road, and managed to paint part of their mascot - a fine-looking billie goat - an unmistakable Dorset grass green. I forget whether the culprits - or heroes, depending on your viewpoint - were ever caught.*

Like Dick Eberlie, Bob recalls the Officers' Mess games. *The Mess was in a couple of corrugated iron, domed huts (Quansets), the ante-room of which was kept reasonably cool by a fan suspended from the ceiling. A popular after dinner game was to divide into two teams, occupy separate ends of the room, and toss an empty can into the fan's revolving blades so that it ricocheted at some speed into the opposing team. As the evening progressed the fan was switched up to maximum speed and a well-thrown can would fly off, dangerously hard and fast. Despite this, I can recall no one being badly hurt.*

Himself one of the Battalion's athletic stars, Bob recalls that, although the Dorsets had had a good record of successes in athletics in Austria, because of the turnover of National Servicemen, by the time they reached Hong Kong only five of the victorious 1952 team remained. Despite this, *first came the 27 Brigade Meeting, which we won, narrowly beating 1 RUR. The Hong Kong Land Forces Championships followed and we outclassed the opposition, beating the runners up (45th Field Regiment, Royal Artillery) by a massive twenty-five points.* The CO, Knocker White, was particularly pleased and wrote in the Regimental Journal: 'The Battalion athletic team completely swept the board in a manner which has not been seen since the old 2nd Battalion took on and defeated the entire French Army of the Rhine in 1929.'

Bob remembers that *most major unit sport was held in the winter months in either Kowloon or over in Hong Kong. Travelling to a rugby match, for instance, would entail a bicycle taxi from the camp to Fan Ling railway station, catching a train to Kowloon, crossing by Star ferry over to Hong Kong, taking a taxi to the* stadium - and hoping to be there about fifteen minutes before kick-off.

Lieutenant Klaus Marx, remembers the 4x440 relay race well. *During training on the circuit I trod on what seemed to me a piece of rubber tubing. After completing another circuit I returned to the spot to find two sergeants with angle irons finishing off a large snake which had chosen to bask in the sun. It reminds me of that verse in Psalm 91 v 13 'You will tread upon the cobra.'*

Corporal Donald Knight had served with the Battalion in Vienna and - with Bob Reep, Dick Eberlie and Klaus Marx - was a member of the winning team in the 440 relay race when the Dorsets won the FARELF Championship. He was also a strong swimmer and, aged sixteen, had won the Boy Scouts' Silver Cross for his gallantry in rescuing someone from drowning in West Bay, Bridport. Donald remembers his National Service as the best two years of his life because they enabled him to swim and play other sports. During his time in Hong Kong he swam from Hong Kong to Kowloon - which he remembers as not a great distance but requiring great effort and care. The tide was so strong that he had to swim far out against it and then back in again as he reached Kowloon.

Sergeant *Spud* Taylor shared Donald's memory of the swimming race between Hong Kong and Kowloon: *...the distance was about half to three quarters of a mile but I cannot really remember. The problem was the current, which was so strong that it could carry one away and the actual distance swum could be four or five miles. Normal shipping business continued throughout the race and the swimmers had to avoid anchored cargo ships, cruise liners and sampans by the dozen. I finished somewhere in the middle of the pack but not at all ashamed by my efforts.*

He also remembered the debilitating heat. *Normal dress in camp was 'bare buff' or in other words shorts, boots, socks and a hat. Anyone on guard or other formal duty had to be dressed in full uniform of course, but a clean starched one would only remain dry for ten minutes before it became stained, limp and soaked with sweat. We changed into clean, dry uniforms four or five times a day, but after a few minutes they would be just as bad as the ones we had just changed out of. In camp we slept under individual mosquito-proof nets, but if one or two of the little beasts got inside it, then a night of misery followed... The continuous high temperature combined with the stifling humidity could produce an irritating rash all over the body... known as 'prickly heat'. ...some... suffered it continuously.*

On the whole though the pleasure outweighed the unpleasant and it was a lovely time. There is something very special about the tropics, especially at night. We could look across the hills and see the lights of distant villages twinkling away. The moon seems larger than it does at home. The tropical vegetation and the sounds of myriads of insects as they chirped, twittered and croaked, all combined with the smell of the plants, made it an experience never to be forgotten. Magic.

Private *Tiddler* Damon from Dorchester joined on a three-year engagement and, after initial training at the Depot, went to Topsham Barracks in Exeter for advanced training. He then embarked on the Troopship *Cheshire* for Hong Kong with Peter Foot from Blandford. On arrival in Hong Kong he was posted to A Company, where he remained until the Battalion went to Korea. Tiddler recalls that, because he was small of stature, it was difficult to get a uniform to fit properly and he therefore never looked immaculately turned out. On one occasion he was sent on Guard Duty to Bird's Hill for a month, but rather than regarding this as a punishment, he enjoyed the experience. His CSM had said "Out of sight out of mind", and this suited Tiddler well enough. Overall he enjoyed his service with the Battalion, adding: *I joined as a lad, and came home a man.*

Corporal Horace Dibben was in B Company with CSM Jimmy James. His particular memory is of the mules which, having wrapped up their hooves to avoid injury, he had to help carry up a steep hill. He recalls with amusement the Dorsets' surprise when a team of Hong Kong bearers arrived to help them carry their supplies up the steep hills. All the lifting was left to the women while the Hong Kong men supervised. One of the women he remembers for her strikingly blue eyes.

Colour Sergeant Ginger Tizzard remembers travelling with a group of Warrant Officers and Sergeants and their wives in an army bus from Kowloon to San Wai camp, where they were to be guests for lunchtime drinks in the Officers' Mess. *At about the halfway mark we were overtaken by a car driven by Captain Archer, accompanied by his wife and Captain Stewart and his wife. Suddenly the car swerved and skidded into a paddy field and overturned. We stopped immediately and several of us managed to break into the car and rescue the occupants. Luckily there were no serious injuries. Everyone seemed to be all right, although badly shaken up, so with a lot of smelly paddy mud and a late arrival we eventually attended the function in the Officers' Mess.*

Ginger still bears the scar in his left eye from an accident during a hammer throwing training session. *The training hammer had a chain instead of a wire and in this instance the chain snapped and a sharp link cut my eyeball, which required treatment in the Military Hospital, Kowloon, resulting in a three-day stay. During this time we were visited in the ward by the Hollywood actor Cary Grant and his newly wedded bride, who were on a visit to Hong Kong on their honeymoon. They shook our hands and were very friendly to chat with. Most thoughtful of them - a very pleasant episode in a rather dreary routine.*

Private Mike Davis-Sellick from Weymouth recalls being teased by his mates for having a double-barrelled surname, which they claimed was a privilege reserved for officers. Because Mike was not quite nineteen years of age when the Battalion left for Korea, he was sent first of all to Battle school in Haremure in Japan, and then to an Australian Signals Unit. The purpose of these postings seems to have been simply to allow Mike to get older because, having reached the age of nineteen, he was posted to rejoin the Dorsets in Korea, where, because of his background in catering, he became the Officers' Mess Caterer.

Private Stan Coombes was in D Company under Captain Steve Elvery. He clearly remembers preparing for the Tattoo, the many rehearsals and having to learn an archaic form of arms drill while the local tailors were kept very busy making the many costumes needed. Sadly Stan was admitted to hospital and missed the Tattoo, but he quickly recovered and soon afterwards was posted on Guard at the Governor's residence. On His Excellency's arrival and the order *Present Arms*, Stan presented arms in the manner of two centuries earlier. Stan says the Governor gave a wry grin, but his Guard Commander was less sympathetic.

Second Lieutenants John Ives and **Bill Tong** arrived in Hong Kong on 29th September 1953 and were posted respectively to B and D Companies. John remembers their being dined in on 22nd October *with all the usual fun and games, including the Bumper Toast.*

At about this time I was summoned by the Adjutant, John Archer, to attend the CO, who when I was marched in said "Jives" - that is what he called me - "I have received an application for you to join the Parachute Regiment. I agreed that I had completed such a form at Sandhurst. He said: "You have just joined the Dorset Regiment." And he tore it up for the waste bin. I never did jump out of an aircraft.

John Ives auctioning the Sarah Sands cake

My next encounter with the CO came after the Sarah Sands Ball of 11th November 1953. At the ball I happened to win the raffle for the iced Sarah Sands cake. I stood up and auctioned the cake, much to the amusement of all the WOs' and Sergeants' guests. I made £15 for the Old Comrades' Association. The day after the ball I was summoned to see the CO. "Jives," he said. "Well done, but don't do it again." I think he felt I had overdone my duties as a young officer.

I thought I would be in the Advance Party to Korea and get my first medal. However, the CO made me Assistant Adjutant to J B Smith. Bill Tong went on the Advance Party and became 'one gong Tong'.

Lance-Corporal Happy Harman joined the Battalion in Hong Kong in November 1953 and, after a spell in D Company, applied to join the Assault Pioneer Platoon under Lt Douglas Jenks and Sgt Johnson. Within a short time Jenks was replaced by Basil Hebden and Johnson by Sgt Spud Taylor, promoted from the Sniper section. The Dorsets were strong on nicknames and Taylor acquired three: Spud, Dusty and (because he habitually told his men *to cut all the waffling*) Waffler.

Happy remembers an incident when the Welch Regiment erected a large sign bearing their unofficial motto - *Stick it The Welch*. On the night of 1st August 1954 a party of Dorsets broke into the Welch Regiment' lines and removed the sign as a trophy. All hell broke loose, the offenders were identified and disciplinary action was begun - which was forgotten in the excitement of the Battalion's imminent departure to Korea.

Two brothers - **Corporal Ron and Private Len Webb** - remember their time with the Battalion. Ron arrived first, serving six years in all with the Dorsets in Austria, Hong Kong and Korea. On arrival at San Wai from the *Empire Fowey*, Ron joined D Company commanded by Major John Drew. During his time he was promoted to corporal and was a reserve for the Battalion's boxing team. After about a year in the Colony, Ron was joined by Len, who arrived aboard the *Empire Trooper*, joining 10 Platoon under Lieutenant John Ives. On the voyage Len made friends with a soldier who had already served in Hong Kong with the Wiltshires. During his first tour, he had fallen in love with a Chinese girl but had returned with his Battalion to the UK. Wanting to be re-united

Corporal Ron Webb   *Private Len Webb on right*

with his girlfriend, he had signed on again, this time with the Dorsets, who he knew were in Hong Kong. Len remembers that, on arrival, he visited her only to discover that she had married someone else and moved away. After this, Len's friend rather regretted having signed on for another three years.

Len enjoyed his time in the New Territories. He recalls the Commanding Officer as *a fitness fanatic who had us on the go all the time. Before the move to Korea the CO told the Battalion that "we might not be the best soldiers in Korea - that's open to debate - but we will be the fittest."*

More than six decades later, almost all of these men are members of the Dorset Regiment's Old Comrades Association. With their comrades who served in Germany and England, they meet often at Branch meetings, anniversaries, dinners and their monthly coffee mornings at the Keep in Dorchester. Today they are in their eighties. Most have whiter hair - or less hair - than once was the case, but their memories of these times remain sharp. Anyone lucky enough to be invited to join one of their gatherings will be left with no doubts about the abiding strength of the ties of shared experience and comradeship that bind them together, or about what it means to be a Dorset.

Appendix 1

The Dorset Regimental Hymn

Our Father, by whose servants
This Regiment was raised,
For all Thy wondrous mercies
Thy Holy name be praised.
For Thine unfailing mercies, Far-
strewn along our way,
With all who passed before us,
We praise Thy name today.

They reap not where they laboured,
We reap what they have sown;
Our harvest may be garnered
By ages yet unknown.
The days of old have dowered us
With gifts beyond all praise;
Our Father, make us faithful
To serve the coming days.

The changeful years unresting
Their silent course have sped,
New comrades ever bringing
In comrades' steps to tread;
And some are long forgotten,
Long spent their hopes and fears,
Safe rest they in Thy keeping,
Who changeth not with years.

Before us and beside us,
Still holden in Thine hand,
A cloud unseen of witness,
Our elder comrades stand:
Our family unbroken,
We join, with one acclaim,
One heart, one voice uplifting,
To glorify Thy name.

Tune Aurelia by Samuel Sebastian Wesley (The Church's one foundation…)

The Dorset Regimental Collect

O Christ, our Redeemer, the sure stronghold of each succeeding age, grant that we, who bear arms in The Dorset Regiment, may endure as our fathers did before us, with steadfast courage. Lead us in every quarter of the earth; that we may not only honour and proclaim Thy Name, but also serve to open a highway for Thy Salvation for all mankind, through the same Jesus Christ, who liveth and reigneth with the Father and the Holy Spirit, one God, world without end. Amen.

(Composed by Captain The Rev Gus Claxton MC RAChD,
Padre of 2nd Battalion 1939-45)

Appendix 2

1st Battalion Order of Battle
December 1952

CO Lt-Col D A Affleck-Graves
2IC Maj R G Hill MBE
Adj Capt A J Archer
IO Lt A C A Wallis
RSM WOI L J Webber
MTO Capt R H B Feltham

QM Capt L T Smithers
RQMS WOII W H Vaughan
ORQMS WOII W A G Ralph MBE
RMO Lt P Boultbee RAMC
Bandmr J Plant

HQ Company
Capt J E G Knight
Lt B J Sims
Lt R A F Reep
2/Lt R A Rowbotham
2/Lt J B Cook
WOII S Wells
C/Sgt P Blissett
CSM J Underwood
CSM H French
C/Sgt Lloyd

B Company
Maj V A J Heald DSO MBE MC
Capt J D Freer-Smith
Lt B G L Hebden
2/Lt G B Blight
2/Lt J D Gilmour
CSM R F James MM
C/Sgt V F Howe

C Company
Capt C A Morris
2/Lt R F Eberlie
2/Lt D B Edwards
2/Lt K Marx
CSM C West
C/Sgt N Carter

D Company
Capt J Drew
Lt A J Smoker
Lt P N Elgar
2/Lt R I C Campbell
CSM L D Pitman
C/Sgt K Marquis

S Company
Maj I F R Ramsay
Capt J F Wreford
Lt M J Reynolds
2/Lt J D F Jenks

2/Lt R J Moylan
CSM Evans
C/Sgt F Glanville

1st Battalion Order of Battle
September 1954

CO Lt-Col O G W White DSO
2IC Maj R H Wheatley DSO
Adj Maj J B Smith
A/Adj 2/Lt J Ives
IO 2/Lt A N Solomons
QM Capt L T Smithers
RMO Lt E C Campbell RAMC
RSM WOI L J Webber

A Company
Capt H L K Jones
Capt W J Guinan
Lt J B St V Hawkins
2/Lt S M Alley
Lt D W Taylor
2/Lt J F C Robb
CSM V F Howe

C Company
Capt A G Jelley
Capt C E K Speller
2/Lt C G C Hosking
2/Lt R A de L H Bembridge
2/Lt J C Rogers
CSM J Russell

S Company
OC Maj J Drew
MMG Lt R A F Reep
A/Tk 2/Lt P S Groom

HQ Company
OC Maj H V Thomas
PRI Maj A A P C Thomas TD
Capt H C Ealand
RSO Lt D B Edwards
MTO Capt R H B Feltham
RQMS WOII W H Vaughan
CSM WOII C Rice

B Company
Capt J B Wreford
Capt E C Stones
Lt J D F Jenks
2/Lt A P Jones
2/Lt I S Foster
2/Lt A F Thompson
CSM R F James MM

D Company
Capt S S Elvery
Capt M J Reynolds
2/Lt P M Merrikin
2/Lt J W Hambly
2/Lt J W Tong
CSM L D Pitman

Mortar Lt A R Tawney
A/Pionr Lt B G L Hebden
CSM WOII K Marquis

Glossary

2 i/c	Second in Command	DOA	Dead on Arrival
2/Lt	Second Lieutenant	DSO	Distinguished Service Order
ADC	Aide de Camp	FARELF	Far Eastern Land Forces
ATS	Auxiliary Territorial Service - women in khaki in the Army	GOC	General Officer Commanding
		HE	His Excellency the Governor
B and H	Bedfordshire and Hertfordshire Regiment	HM	His/Her Majesty
		HMS	His/Her Majesty's Ship
Bedfs and Herts	Bedfordshire and Hertfordshire Regiment	HQ	Headquarters
		HRH	His/Her Royal Highness
BMH	British Military Hospital	IS	Internal Security
Capt	Captain	JG	Jungle green uniform
CB	Confined to Barracks	KOSB	King's Own Scottish Borderers
CinC	Commander in Chief	Lt or Lieut	Lieutenant
CO	Commanding Officer	LMG	Light Machine Gun or Bren gun
Col	Colonel		
Compradore	Kitchen Manager	Lt Col	Lieutenant Colonel
Cpl	Corporal	MC	Military Cross
CQMS	Company Quartermaster Sergeant	MO	Medical Officer
		NAAFI	Navy, Army and Air Force Institute
C/Sgt	Colour Sergeant		
CSM	Company Sergeant Major	NCO	Non-commissioned Officer
DCLI	Duke of Cornwall's Light Infantry	OCTU	Officer Cadet Training Unit
		OG	Olive green uniform
DF	Defensive Fire	OP	Observation Post
DJ	Dinner jacket	OS	Old Shirburnian
DLI	Durham Light Infantry	PIAT	Anti-tank Infantry Projector

PMC	President of Mess Committee
PT	Physical training
Pte	Private soldier
RA	Royal Artillery
RAF	Royal Air Force
RASC	Royal Army Service Corps
REME	Royal Electrical and Mechanical Engineers
RFC	Royal Flying Corps
RUR	Royal Ulster Rifles
RSM	Regimental Sergeant Major
SS	Steam Ship
TA	Territorial Army
TAB	Typhoid A & B vaccine
TEWT	Tactical exercise without troops
TMB	Trench Mortar Battery
USRC	United Services Recreation Club
WOSB	War Office Selection Board

Index

PB indicates that the person appears in a photograph in the block between pages 148 and 149

Adams, Cpl 72
Affleck-Graves, Lt Col Tom 3, 8, 44, 57, 58
Archer, Capt John 4, 45, 51, 55, 88, 125, 138, 143, PB, 162, 163
Archer, Marie 55, 125
Ayling, Sgt 68
Baldwin, Pte 139
Ball Lt Col Os 12
Ballard, Cpl 70
Barlow, 2/Lt David 33
Barnes, Pte Darky 139
Barton, Cpl Michael 14-15, 157-8
Beales, Pte Edwin 146
Blight, 2/Lt Gerald 45-6, 97, 101, 104, 113, 115, 119, 121, 141, PB
Blundell, Lt Alan 3, 142
Boddy, Cpl 145, PB
Boultbee, Dr Peter 46, 63, 115
Brain, Pte Cocoa PB
Bredin, Lt Col Speedy 12
Brookes, Sgt 60
Bryant, Pte John 150
Burgess, Pte Patrick 5-6

Campbell, 2/Lieut Dick 46, 123, 130, PB
Carter, C/Sgt Nick 146
Carver, Officer Cadet Robin 27
Casey, Pte later 2/Lt Mike 22, 27
Cavell, Mr 12
Challacombe, Pte F PB
Chandler, Pte Harry 150
Chang, the Chinese boy 60
Chant, Pte Dave 149, 150
Chappell, Cpl 84
Chettle, Capt Clive 144
Cobbold, 2/Lt Mike 33
Coombes, Pte Stan 163
Crane, Cpl 121, 145, 146, PB
Creech, C/Sgt Fred 31, 37, 66, 69, PB
Curl, Pte John PB, 153-5
Damon, Pte Tiddler 162
Dartnall, Capt Darts 33, 36, 149
Dashwood, 2/Lt Mike 21
Davis-Sellick, Pte Mike 163
Dibben, Cpl Horace 16, 143, 145, 162
Dodds, Padre Lee 46, 99, 101

173

Drew, Capt John 46, 55, 59, 70, 74-6, 79, 83, 99, 120, PB, 165
Drew, Mrs Maisie 46, 55, 99
Drysdale, Andrew, Officer Cadet 27, 29
Dudley, 2/Lt John 33
Dutton, Alan & family 127
Ealand, Capt Tim 36, 76, 101, 111, PB
Ealand, Mrs Anne 101, 111
Eavis, Pte Geoff 18, 155-6
Eberlie, Lt Dick *passim*
Eberlie, Susan 87
Eckersall, L/Cpl Jeff 15-16, 152-3
Edmonds, Pte Dilly 153
Edward-Collins, Lt 33
Edwards, Lt Brian 45, 99, 121, 134, PB
Elgar, Lt Peter 46, PB
Elgie, Sgt Norman 147
Ellis, Laurence, Officer Cadet 27
Elvery, Capt Steve 36-7, 86, 107-8, 143, PB, 163
England, Pte John 153
Farminer, Sgt Vic 156
Fellowes, Sgt J 134
Feltham, Capt Bob 45, PB
Fields, Sgt Gracie 153-4, 156
Foot, Pte Edgar 139
Foulger, Cpl 68
Freer-Smith, Capt John 4, 6, 45, 159
Freer-Smith, Mrs Angela 45
Freeth, Cpl 118, 121
Frost, Pte Titch 153
Gaye, Lt Col Douglas 33
George, Pte 72
Gilmore, 2/Lt John 45
Given, Sgt Jock 144

Glover, Lt Col Peter & Mrs Wendy 130
Gordon, Pte 60, PB
Gough, Cpl F 134
Graham, Pte PB
Hall, Bishop of Hong Kong 147
Hall, Maj Henry 143, PB
Hands, Pte then 2/Lt Ray 21-2
Harman, L/Cpl Happy 156, 164-5
Hawkins, Lt Brian 108, PB
Heald, Maj Bill 3, 65, 70, 97, 107, 123-6
Hebden, Lt Basil 45, PB, 164
Hedger, Cllr Edward 12
Hill, Maj Reggie 44, 51, 95, 117
Hill, Maj Roly 33
Hill, Mr 114
Hill, Mrs Doris 44, 117
Hobbs, Cpl 84
Hobbs, RSM 142
Hodgkins, Pte 72
Home, Lt Gos 158-9
Hosking, Lt Jimmy 145, PB
Howe, CSM Vic PB
Ives, Lt John 163, 164, 165
James, CSM Jimmy 4, 135, 144, PB, 162
Jelley, Capt Tony 137, 146, PB, 149, 153-6
Jenks, Lt Douglas 45, 92, 96, 101, 108, PB, 164
Judd, Pte R 72, PB
Kent, HRH Duchess of 108-9, 124, 135
Knight, Betty 45, 50
Knight, Capt John 45
Knight, Cpl Donald 122, PB, 161
Lane, Pte Peter 153
Laugher, Lt Col Skinny 12
Lavers, Pte 60

Lawless, Pte M 146
Leach, Sgt 70, 84
Lewers, 2/Lt Ben 27, 33
Little, Anne 42
Little, Pte Bob PB
Little, Roger 25
Lloyd C/Sgt Marie 135
Loewen, Lt Gen Sir Charles 139, 143
Long, Pte 93, 124
MacDonald, Capt Scott 27
Maers, Pte Stan 153
Marquis, CSM Ken PB, 154
Marsh, Pte Tony 149, 150, 157
Marx, 2/Lt Klaus 45, 120, 122, PB, 161
Metcalfe, Sgt Len 4
Miller, Cpl 145
Milner, Lt John 3
Morris, Maj Tony 45, 134, 135, 143, 147, PB
Morris, Mr 12
Moylan, 2/Lt Ross 46, 59, 123
Munday, Pte Robert 146
Nixon, Senator Richard 137, 138
Norris, Pte Pat 150
Osmond, Pte Bill PB
Pattenden, Cpl 60, 70, 84
Pearmain, 2/Lt Peter 59, 88, 107
Phillips, Pte C 134, PB
Plant, Bandmaster John 124, 135, 142, 145, PB
Pollock, Cpl Polly 72
Pratten, Pte Gordon 155
Pugsley, Sgt 31, 37
Purvis, Pte 60
Ralph, ORQMS Ted 4, 146, 147, PB

Ramsay, Maj Ivor 4, 12, 46, 70, 85, 102, 124, PB, 149, 151, 153
Rawlings, Pte later Sgt 41
Read, Pte Frank 151-2
Reep, Lt Bob 14, 45, 118-19, 122, 134, PB, 160-1
Reynolds, Capt John 45, 99, 125, PB
Reynolds, Mrs Jocelyn, 45, 99
Richards Mr 12
Robertson Sgt C 134, 135
Robertson, Mrs 113
Ross-Skinner, Col Harry & Mrs 42
Rowbotham, 2/Lt Dick 45, 59, 70, 75-6, 83-4
Rowland, Pte Ken PB
Sandford, Pte Bert PB
Sheppard, Pte Roy PB, 156
Shortis, Lt Colin 5, 158-60
Sims, Capt John 45, 65
Sinnick, Pte D 134
Smith, Capt JB 4, 143, PB, 164
Smithers, Capt [QM] Slick 140, PB
Smoker, Lt John 46, PB
Spinks, Florence Mary 43
Stanley, Pte Abe 134
Stephenson, Col Steve 12
Stevens, Mr 12
Stewart, Capt Geoff 143, PB, 162
Stirling, Brig Bill 16
Stride, Pte 47
Sugden, Lt Gen Sir Cecil 147
Suter, Pte 72
Symes, Lt Col Sam 12
Taylor, Sgt Spud 9-13, 16-17, 161-2, 164
Thomas, D/M Tommy 145, PB
Tizzard, Sgt Ginger PB, 162-3

Tong, Lt Bill PB, 164-5
Tourtel, L/Cpl 147, PB
Trodd, CSM Mick 135, PB
Trowbridge, L/Cpl PB
Urquhart, Brigadier Tiger 16
Vaughan, RQMS Jackie 135, 138, PB
Wallis, Lt Charles 45, 73-4
Ward, Lt Gen Sir Dudley 139-40
Wareham, Pte 93
Way, Pte PB
Webb, Cpl Ron 84, 165
Webb, Pte Len 165, 166
Webber, 2/Lt John 37-8
Webber, RSM John 4, 33, 36, 44, 62, 135, PB, 153
Wheatley, Maj Rupert 4, 145, PB
Whiffen, Pte Paddy PB
White, Lt Col Knocker *passim*
Williams, Maj Morris PB, 154
Wood, Lt-Col Tim 8, 12
Wood, Maj Gen G N 39-40
Woodhouse, Brig Charles 12
Worrall, Maj Dennis 36, 38
Wreford, Capt John 46, PB, 149, 153
Wreford, Mrs Jo 46, 149, 153
Wynne-Griffiths, 2/Lt David 33